G000134384

HANNIBAL AND SCIPIO

POCKET
GIANTS

HANNIBAL AND SCIPIO

POCKET GIANTS

GREG
FISHER

The
History
Press

For my parents

Cover images © Mary Evans Picture Library

First published 2016

The History Press
The Mill, Brimscombe Port
Stroud, Gloucestershire, GL5 2QG
www.thehistorypress.co.uk

© Greg Fisher, 2016

The right of Greg Fisher to be identified as the Author
of this work has been asserted in accordance with the
Copyright, Designs and Patents Act 1988.

All rights reserved. No part of this book may be reprinted
or reproduced or utilised in any form or by any electronic,
mechanical or other means, now known or hereafter invented,
including photocopying and recording, or in any information
storage or retrieval system, without the permission in writing
from the Publishers.

British Library Cataloguing in Publication Data.
A catalogue record for this book is available from the British Library.

ISBN 978 0 7509 5590 4

Typesetting and origination by The History Press
Printed and bound in Malta, by Melita Press.

Contents

Please note: all dates are BC, unless otherwise stated.

Map

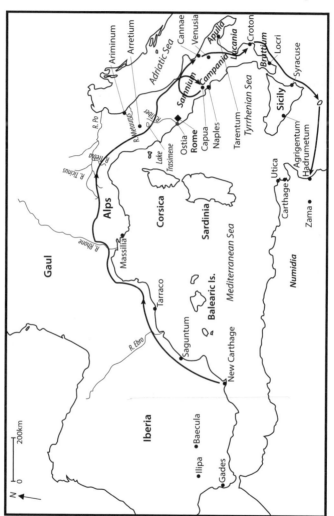

The western Mediterranean in the time of the Hannibalic War. The arrow marks Hannibal's journey. (Illustration by Aaron Styba)

Main Characters

Romans

The Scipio Family

(1) Publius Cornelius Scipio, consul 218, father of Scipio Africanus
(2) Gnaeus Cornelius Scipio, consul 222, brother of (1)
(3) Publius Cornelius Scipio 'Africanus', consul 205 and 194
(4) Lucius Cornelius Scipio 'Asiaticus', brother of (3)
(5) Publius Cornelius Scipio Aemilianus, grandson by adoption of (3), patron of Polybius

It is anachronistic to call (3) 'Africanus' before 201; to avoid confusion (1) and (2) are called the 'elder Scipios' or 'the Scipio brothers' and (3) the 'younger Scipio'.

Other Leaders

Aemilius Paullus, consul 216
Cato the Elder, enemy of the Scipios
Claudius Nero, consul 207
Crispinus, consul 208
Fabius Maximus, dictator in 217

Flamininus, conqueror of Macedonia
Flaminius, consul 217
Fulvius Flaccus, general
Laelius, lieutenant of Africanus
Livius Salinator, consul 207
Marcellus, killed 208
Marcius, Roman commander in Spain
Minucius, Fabius' second in command
Sempronius, consul 218
Servilius, consul 217
Silanus, lieutenant of Africanus
Tiberius Gracchus, son-in-law of Africanus
Varro, consul 216

Carthaginians

The Barcid Family

(1) Hamilcar Barca, father of Hannibal; died in Spain, 228
(2) Hasdrubal 'The Fair', son-in-law of (1); killed 221
(3) Hannibal, son of (1), invader of Italy
(4) Hanno, nephew of (3)
(5) Hasdrubal, brother of (3), general; killed 207
(6) Mago, brother of (3), general; died 203

Other Leaders

Bomilcar, general
Hanno, anti-Barcid politician
Hasdrubal, 'son of Gisgo'
Marhabal, lieutenant of Hannibal

Other Major Figures

Antiochus III 'The Great', King of Syria
Archimedes, mathematician
Edeco, Spanish nobleman
Eumenes II, King of Pergamum
Hieronymus, anti-Roman King of Syracuse
Indibilis, rebellious Spanish chief
Mandonius, rebellious Spanish chief
Massinissa, Numidian king
Philip V, King of Macedonia
Prusias I, King of Bithynia
Pyrrhus of Epirus, Greek warrior king
Syphax, Numidian king

Introduction

'The Most Memorable War'

I am about to tell the story of the most memorable war of any ever fought – the war that the Carthaginians, under the leadership of Hannibal, waged against Rome.

Livy, 21.1

For nearly all of its 500 years in existence, the Roman Republic was at war. The most famous of all these conflicts was the marathon struggle for supremacy with Carthage between 264 and 146 BC. The principal act of this rivalry was the so-called 'Hannibalic War' or Second Punic War (218–202), which was dominated by two generals: Hannibal Barca of Carthage and the Roman aristocrat Publius Cornelius Scipio Africanus.

Carthage, a Phoenician (in Latin, 'Punic') colony, was based around the city of the same name, now a UNESCO World Heritage Site in Tunisia. At various times Carthage commanded broad swathes of territory across the North African coastline and extended its influence to the islands of the Mediterranean. The Roman Republic, created in *c.* 509 when the last king of Rome was ejected, had emerged from its humble beginnings as a small village to dominate most of the other communities of Italy. Both states had a powerful aristocracy, and both possessed a formidable military reputation.

The Hannibalic War was Rome's first major Mediterranean conflict. Its generals, soldiers and diplomats saw action over a vast area, including Spain, Macedonia, Greece, Africa, Italy and Sicily. Narrowly escaping extermination in 216, the Romans finally emerged triumphant in 202 after one of the most improbable revivals in military history. This resurgence showed the Mediterranean world the power of Roman arms, laying the foundation for one of the most critical events in world history; with Carthage humbled, Rome steadily conquered the Mediterranean and built an empire that lasted, in various guises, for well over 1,000 years.

The Hannibalic War is filled with courageous deeds, disastrous exhibitions of hubris, and larger-than-life characters. A number of Roman generals, such as Marcellus, Fabius Maximus, Claudius Nero and the elder Scipios, helped Rome to recover from the depths of despair. On the other side, Hannibal's brother Hasdrubal and another Hasdrubal, 'son of Gisgo', together with a number of others, won important victories and earned the praise of the historians who chronicled their deeds. Despite the existence of all of these great figures, Hannibal and Scipio have remained the most famous actors in the story. The second-century BC historian Polybius called the Romans 'true athletes of warfare',[1] but their vaunted armies succumbed repeatedly to Hannibal, earning him a place in legend as Rome's most dangerous enemy.[2] Scipio's successes on the battlefield gave him an unrivalled military reputation, and his contributions in Spain made Rome's triumph possible.

Hannibal and Scipio are examples of 'great individuals': those who, by sheer force of character, their ability to lead and understand the men around them, and their self-belief, courage and political stamina, change the course of history.[3] They have left an indelible impact in the annals of human endeavour as illustrations of the heights of success that personal determination can bring. Their effect on history can also be measured in the way they inspired others. Hannibal's tactics encouraged generations of military leaders, including such luminaries as Napoleon Bonaparte. Scipio's place as the most famous Roman hero of the Republican era later earned his name a place in Italy's national anthem and (less enviably) as a poster boy in Mussolini's revival of Italian power in the 1930s. In the film *Scipione l'africano* (director C. Gallone, 1937), Scipio (played by the suitably named Annibale Ninchi), triumphing over the 'African' Carthaginians, was used to justify Italian imperialist ambitions in Africa. Both men have often been taken out of their historical context and used for a whole host of purposes, a feat made possible only by the 'brand recognition' they earned from their deeds in antiquity.

The war attracts a range of other modern comparisons. In particular, the long prelude to the Hannibalic War bears more than a passing resemblance to the interwar period in the twentieth century: the harsh treatment of a defeated enemy, the emergence of a new political elite, rearmament and then finally a 'guarantee' – in this case, the Roman friendship given to the Spanish city of Saguntum – that was no guarantee at all. Hannibal's invasion of Italy, with its long supply lines and his inability to match the numbers of his enemy, has drawn comparisons with the disastrous invasions of Russia by both Hitler and Napoleon.

Hannibal and Scipio serve as signal illustrations of the fine line between success and failure. Hannibal's brilliant victories over Rome at the River Trebia (218), Lake Trasimene (217) and Cannae (216) were followed by years of near-imprisonment in southern Italy. Hannibal also angered the Carthaginian aristocracy, who later tried to blame him for the war as they desperately negotiated for peace with Rome. After a brief stint in politics, Hannibal once more turned against Rome, but failing again, took poison as Roman agents closed in on his position. Scipio helped to mastermind the astonishing revival which laid the foundation for Hannibal's defeat, but then found himself eased out of Roman politics, exiled from the state he had saved. Ironically, both men fell from grace and died at around the same time.[4]

Hannibal and Scipio also had a sizeable impact on a major political process that forever changed the Mediterranean world: the collapse of corporate rule and the emergence of a new Roman monarchy. For much of the Republican era, the Roman constitution – whose structure of checks and balances against the abuse of power by any single part of government inspired the American political system – ensured that the ambitions of the individual were channelled into the service of the state. No one man was allowed to accumulate excess power, and elected officials typically served in collegial, not single positions. For example, two men, rather than one, were elected each year to serve as 'consul', the highest office in the state responsible for military, civil and religious matters. Service as consul was the pinnacle of an aristocratic career. In the role of consul, members of the Roman elite defeated Rome's enemies on the battlefield, presided over sacrifices for the health of the state and helped the Senate set policy, earning *gloria* – social and political renown – in the process. Only through service to the state could *gloria* be won. Following their year in office, consuls moved on to other positions, retired or joined the Senate. Although Carthage also had a republican system of government, its leaders – men like Hannibal and his family – looked more like Hellenistic warrior-kings than Roman consuls. Winning glory had less to do with the needs of the state, and more to do with the development of a personality cult, supported by the favour of the gods. These kings became celebrities through their wartime exploits and used propaganda to nurture their reputation. Famous examples of this archetype include most of the successors to Alexander the Great, such as Pyrrhus of Epirus, who invaded Italy and was beaten by the Romans in 275 after a bloody struggle.[5]

These two competing visions of political authority collided in the third-century BC Mediterranean. Neither Pyrrhus nor Hannibal, strong and charismatic individuals though they were, could outlast the incredible corporate strength of the Roman Republic. Polybius saw Roman tenacity as a product of its constitution, whose layers of collegial offices, tempered by the will of the people and the oversight of the Senate, restrained dangerous individualism and provided an unbeatable resilience. Yet, despite its depth, this system did not survive its encounter with Hannibal intact. Rome's catastrophic defeats between 218 and 216 exposed cracks in the corporate system and called for a Roman version of the individualistic hero – Scipio –

to overwhelm Hannibal's charisma, leadership and divine favour. When the war was over, however, the rather unnatural amounts of power that Scipio had accumulated in the process aroused feelings of trepidation amongst Rome's political elite. Scipio had personally forged a mighty army which had served with him and his family for seven years, and he richly rewarded them after the war ended. Scipio encouraged rumours about divine support and became a talisman for the Roman cause. Instead of blending into the constitutional framework, Scipio, like Hannibal, had become a recognisable brand in military and political circles, earning admiration and suspicion in equal measure. There are similarities between Scipio and the warlords of the late Republic – men like Julius Caesar – who broke free of Rome's 'duty-first' corporate mentality. Scipio's victory over Hannibal moved the Republic one step closer to the political and social revolution of Caesar's time, where a civil war raged across the Mediterranean. Within a generation of his murder in 44, Caesar's great-nephew Octavian – better known to history as Augustus – reigned supreme over the Roman world.

The Hannibalic War stands at the pivot of several important events in world history: the steady march from Republic to Empire, the eventual rise of a Roman imperial monarchy and the systematic collapse of any opposition to Roman power in the Mediterranean. Given its importance, it is remarkable that hardly any contemporary evidence for the war and its two leading generals has survived. The most influential account of the war, that of Livy (59 BC–AD 17), was actually written about two centuries after the events. Writing under the patronage of Augustus, Livy told the story of the war as part of a grand effort to write an all-inclusive history of Rome. His views about the Roman past were, though, deeply skewed by the collapse of the Republic. Livy could remember the bloody struggle for political supremacy that took the lives of Julius Caesar, Pompey, Antony and Cleopatra. Roman society was torn apart by the civil war, and as Livy assembled his *History of Rome*, he searched the past for tales of heroism, piety, courage and moral fortitude to provide encouragement for his troubled world. Conveniently, all of these inspirational virtues could be found in Scipio's victory over Hannibal, which Livy – with a fair knowledge of such celebrated struggles as the Persian invasion of Greece and the conflict between Athens and Sparta not long afterwards – soberly presented to his audience as 'the most memorable war' of all time. Livy turned the tale of Rome's victory in the Second Punic War into a patriotic morality play, showing how a pious, dutiful people, fused together under the leadership of the Senate and its generals, prevailed over incredible odds. To accomplish this task, Livy took no small measure of artistic licence, inventing speeches and using a whole host of literary devices. His version of the contest between Hannibal and Scipio remains a gripping read but cannot be considered an objective history of events.[6]

Although he barely mentions him by name, one of Livy's main sources was the Greek politician Polybius. Born shortly after the Roman victory over Hannibal,

Polybius was much closer to the action than Livy and was able to conduct interviews with survivors of the war and to visit its battlefields. Polybius was once a leading statesman in a southern Greek confederation known as the Achaean League. When Rome's relations with the league turned sour in the early second century, Polybius was deported to Rome as a political hostage. There, he won the friendship of a man named Scipio Aemilianus who had impeccable political credentials: he was the grandson of the consul Aemilius Paullus, killed in Hannibal's great victory at Cannae in 216, and by adoption, he was also the grandson of Scipio Africanus himself. Polybius flourished in the world of the Roman power elite, where he wrote one of the most important books of antiquity. This work, the *Histories*, sought to explain the rapid and incredible Roman conquest of the Mediterranean. The *Histories* only survives in fragments for the period after 216, but represents a significant systematic attempt to write what we might think of as an analytical history.[7]

Livy and Polybius aside, our other sources for the Hannibalic War and its two leading figures are sparse. Roman sources include the aristocrat Fabius Pictor, whose partisan history in Greek survives only in fragments; the politician Alimentus, who was captured by Hannibal; the famous statesman Cato the Elder (234–149), who served under Scipio and later became his political enemy (see Chapter 7); and a certain Gaius Acilius, who was writing in the mid-second century BC. Hannibal, and the war in general, are mentioned to varying degrees in the work of Diodorus Siculus (*c.* 90–*c.* 29), Pompeius Trogus (*fl.* during the reign of Augustus), Appian of Alexandria (*c.* AD 95–165) and Cassius Dio (*c.* AD 155–235), among other later writers.[8] Two other works, the *Punica* of Silius Italicus, a 12,000-verse Latin poem written in the first century AD, and the *Annales* of Ennius also dealt with the war. Cornelius Nepos (*c.* 110–24) provides a very short account of Hannibal's life in his *On Great Men*. Unfortunately, the great biographer of antiquity, Plutarch (*c.* AD 50–*c.* 120) did not write a life of Hannibal; he may have written a biography of Scipio, but if he did, it has vanished. Scipio apparently wrote several works, including a letter to King Philip V of Macedon about his victories in Spain, but nothing appears to have survived even into the century after his death. Like Alexander the Great, Hannibal employed expedition historians, Silenus, a Sicilian, and a Spartan named Sosylus, to chronicle his exploits, but their writings are only known from later writers. Sosylus, as well as a Greek writer, Chaereas, are disparaged by Polybius, who dismisses their work as 'the common gossip of the barber shop'.[9]

All of this means that any history of the Hannibalic War and its leading generals depends on a very one-sided set of historical sources, written by the victors of the conflict. Even these triumphant texts are incomplete, biased or full of problems. As we shall see, Hannibal and Scipio defy simple characterisation, remaining two of the most elusive celebrities of the ancient world. Yet both offer valuable lessons: how can success so rapidly turn into abject and total failure? How can a people be welded together to face insurmountable odds? What makes a great military commander? What constitutes strong political leadership? Some of the answers to these questions are found in the lives of Hannibal Barca and Scipio Africanus.

1

Phony War

Of all that befell both nations, Romans and Carthaginians, the cause was one man and one mind – Hannibal.

Polybius, 9.22

In 264 BC, the Roman people, flushed with confidence from the recent victory over Pyrrhus, threw their weight behind a consular proposal to send an expeditionary force to Sicily to 'help out' a beleaguered group of Italian mercenaries. Despite efforts to avoid antagonising Carthage, which had significant interests in western Sicily, once the Romans made landfall the original mission was quickly jettisoned in favour of grander objectives, and a full-blown conflict erupted. The struggle for Sicily became known as the First Punic War, and only ended in 241 when the Carthaginian navy suffered a catastrophic defeat. The causes of the Hannibalic War are to be found in the murky period following the Carthaginian surrender.

The First Punic War bred a great deal of resentment at Carthage. Already exhausted by the long conflict, Carthage was then hit by a huge war indemnity. The state was bankrupt and unable to pay its mercenaries, who quickly revolted. As the government tried to stave off their attack, the Romans opportunistically snatched Sardinia from Carthaginian control, adding to Carthaginian humiliation. A growing number of the elite determined to rebuild Carthage and rescue it from this misfortune.

Key in this group was Hamilcar Barca, father of Hannibal and head of the influential Barcid clan. He had watched the Carthaginian defeat unfold from his fortified eyrie at Mount Eryx in Sicily; stranded by the surrender of the navy, he had no choice but to follow suit. The future faced by the Barcids and their allies looked grim, with Carthage hamstrung by reparations, and the outlook in North Africa bleak.

A more promising prospect lay in Spain. The Iberian Peninsula possessed abundant manpower and raw materials, and was well away from even the nearest Roman outposts. With a young Hannibal in tow, Hamilcar set out for Spain to begin the long process of restoring Carthaginian fortunes. There, he built a war chest and an army of Spanish militia to serve alongside soldiers recruited from North Africa. The gamble worked and not only helped to drag Carthage out of the despair caused by its defeat, but also cemented the position of Hamilcar and his family as the new Carthaginian elite.

According to popular tradition, the Barcid mission in Spain was fuelled by an implacable hatred of the Roman Republic. The most famous story of the time claims that when Hannibal was just 9, Hamilcar took the young boy to a routine sacrifice. There, he made him swear before the gods to be the eternal, unremitting enemy of Rome. Polybius recounts this vignette in the context of Hannibal's much later attempt to prove his anti-Roman bona fides to Antiochus III, King of Syria, to whom he had fled for sanctuary. Antiochus was on the wrong side of Rome by that point, and Hannibal saw an opportunity to establish his credentials.[10]

Hamilcar died in 229/8, and was succeeded by Hasdrubal 'The Fair', Hannibal's brother-in-law.

According to Roman sources, Hasdrubal continued what Hamilcar had started, stoking the anti-Roman fires among the Carthaginians, reserving special attention for Hannibal. Hasdrubal succumbed to what Polybius calls 'self-seeking ambition and lust for power',[11] and the Romans liked to think that this rubbed off on Hannibal, turning him into an anti-Roman autocrat who nurtured an unquenchable thirst for vengeance.

Roman sources blamed the Hannibalic War almost entirely on Hannibal's lust for revenge, casting him as *the* anti-Roman nemesis who nearly exterminated them.[12] This negative view is a little too convenient, and it is misleading to see Hannibal or even the Barcids as the major factor in bringing Rome and Carthage to war. For one thing, the Barcid dynasty might have increasingly charted their own course in Spain, but they still took some of their policy cues from the Carthaginian Senate.[13] For another, it is just as easy to find fault with Rome, whose seizure of Sardinia and treatment of Carthage at the end of the first conflict were hardly calculated to ensure peace. Policy hawks in the Roman Senate were wary of any Carthaginian resurgence, and Barcid activities in Spain were a cause for concern. Polybius, in an elegant discussion of who was really responsible for the Hannibalic War, states that it is possible to find fault with both parties.[14]

As the Barcids cemented their gains, tensions between Rome and Carthage escalated, and before long a phony war began, with Spain as its focus. In 226, a Roman delegation made a wary agreement with Hasdrubal 'The Fair', to determine Roman and Carthaginian spheres of influence in the peninsula. Carthage and Rome had developed numerous treaties of this kind in the past, even before they went to war; this newer version decided that Carthage would not make any armed moves north of the River Ebro. By implication – although it is not clear if this was ever actually stated anywhere – Rome would not cross to the *south* of the Ebro. In theory, this treaty ensured that both states would avoid the affairs of the other.

Polybius suggests, however, that this new treaty was not simply designed to maintain a peaceful status quo. Penning Hasdrubal south of the Ebro was instead a delaying tactic, because the Romans had finally realised that the Barcids were rather too successful in Spain, where they had won over numerous communities, recruited a large number of soldiers and gained access to crucial raw materials like metals and wood. While some in the Roman Senate were alarmed that all this would soon be directed towards Italy and urged action, others counselled against a hasty response. There were security problems closer to home, in northern Italy and along the Adriatic coast. Both of these areas were subjected to Roman operations immediately prior to the war with Hannibal, strongly suggesting that the Roman Senate had measured and prioritised the threats to the state. Ranking the Barcids as the most significant threat, they tied up loose ends closer to home before tackling the real issue in Spain.[15] For now, Hasdrubal could stay south of the Ebro, while the Romans quietly made their own preparations.

For the latter part of the 220s, Carthaginian power in Spain continued to grow, while the Romans studiously avoided triggering a war with the Barcids.[16] In 221, Hannibal assumed the Carthaginian command after Hasdrubal was murdered, and it was likely that whatever 'hatred' he felt for Rome was by then receiving ample encouragement from the Romans themselves. Speaking of the final phase of the posturing that characterised the phony war, Polybius says that it was 'clear to anyone with an open mind' that Rome and Carthage would soon be locked in a far more serious conflict.[17]

The event that ended the phony war and brought both states into open conflict was Hannibal's siege of the Spanish city of Saguntum in 219. This city was a Roman friend, but it lay in the Carthaginian sphere of influence south of the Ebro. The date of the Roman friendship with Saguntum has been hotly debated for many years and remains uncertain.[18] It is a crucial matter, because the friendship with Saguntum, by which Rome was obliged to render assistance if the city fell into trouble, was rather unrealistic; given the vast distances involved, there could never have been any serious prospect of direct intervention should the city be attacked. It is therefore possible that Rome's 'friendship' with Saguntum was designed to create a pretext for war. The Romans were always careful to ensure their aggression was legal, and many of their most successful conflicts – the First Punic War included – were prompted by requests for help from their 'friends'. Roman 'friendships' were guaranteed by the gods, and inaction when a friend was in trouble was unacceptable. (Action, on the other hand, frequently resulted in the Romans gaining land, plunder, slaves, power, and so on.) In this particular case, allowing Saguntum to burn to the ground while Roman embassies 'protested' – but then seeking a swift and brutal revenge when such protestations came to nothing – might just be a remarkably convenient way to wrap up some unfinished business left by the First Punic War. We may never know what really happened. Roman sources are confused about most aspects of the Saguntine affair, probably reflecting attempts to conceal a whole range of inconvenient truths.[19]

Before the siege began, the people of Saguntum sent ambassadors to Rome to inform their ally that they were increasingly isolated and needed help. Hannibal's constant campaigning south of the Ebro, by which he was simply continuing the policies carried out by his father Hamilcar and brother-in-law Hasdrubal 'The Fair', had left the Saguntines concerned. A Roman embassy was dispatched. Meeting with Hannibal, it warned him to leave Saguntum alone and, for good measure, reminded him of the Ebro treaty. Hannibal, by now conducting siege operations against Saguntum, responded by telling the Roman ambassadors that the city was threatening his own friends in Spain, and so his hostile actions against the city were perfectly legitimate.

Gaining little, the Roman ambassadors left for Carthage, and Hannibal intensified his efforts at Saguntum. In Carthage, the Romans met a frosty reception, and the only party to speak against the looming conflict, Hanno, was rebuffed. With all the benefits of hindsight, Roman tradition casts Hanno as a realist who understood the likely result of a new war with Rome. Saguntum was eventually taken after a long siege; Livy, keen to amplify the betrayal of the city, claims the leading citizens burned themselves to death.[20] Eventually, a new Roman embassy met with the Carthaginian Senate. By now, the damage was done, and there was little to discuss. When the Roman ambassador offered war, the Carthaginian statesmen roared their approval, and the Hannibalic War had begun.

2

Hannibal Ascendant

It is no easy thing to state the truth about him.

Polybius, 9.22

In 219, Hannibal stood on the cusp of three incredible years of unparalleled achievement that would bring the Roman Republic to the edge of extinction. The young man had been raised in war alongside his father Hamilcar and his brother-in-law Hasdrubal 'The Fair' and was supported in his campaigns by a talented entourage of Carthaginian officers and his brothers, Hasdrubal and Mago. Most ancient ideas about Hannibal can be traced back to Polybius, but even he found it hard to disentangle fact and fiction, such was the fame and notoriety of the Carthaginian general in antiquity.[21] Hannibal was a legend, and a talisman for anti-Roman causes.

Nepos reports that Hannibal was well educated and fluent in Greek, a skill useful with the populations of Sicily and southern Italy, which included many of Greek colonial heritage.[22] Unsurprisingly, Hannibal was tough: Cassius Dio says that he had been inured to hardship, was conditioned to endure little sleep and was a man of restrained appetites.[23] Livy states that he was hard-working, and that because of his family name, his resemblance to Hamilcar and his instinctive leadership abilities, he easily won the respect of his soldiers. He was exceptionally brave and determined in battle, and untiring in support of his troops. His acumen for terrain, camouflage and battlefield deception was unparalleled, and he willingly shared the privations of his soldiers.[24] Polybius saw in him an efficient and cool-headed commander,[25] a practical man who gathered intelligence effectively.[26] He had a knack for boosting the confidence of his men during hard times and was not afraid to abandon plans and make new ones when the situation demanded flexibility. This trait, in particular, gave him a valuable edge over the rigid tactical straitjacket of most of his Roman enemies.[27]

The same authors who lavished such praise on his leadership qualities also highlighted the faults they perceived in him. Hannibal was cruel and dishonest and disregarded oath making and treaties.[28] This last characteristic offers a stereotyped idea of the 'perfidious barbarian', in contrast to civilised Roman valour and honour; indeed, 'Punic perfidy' became a negative catch-all in Rome in later years. Polybius sees in him an occasional 'irrational and uncontrollable anger', which Polybius thought clouded his judgement,[29] and accuses him of being overly fond of money.[30]

In 219, this intelligent, complex and dangerous man embarked on one of the most celebrated journeys in history: the crossing of the Alps. The incredibly risky venture was made necessary by Roman naval dominance. In invading Italy, Hannibal's most important strategic challenge was how to negate Rome's significant advantages in manpower. Polybius (via Fabius Pictor) cites the Roman census of 225, attributing nearly 700,000 foot and 70,000 horse to the Roman alliance network, a force made up of the levies of Roman citizens and their Italian allies.[31]

More sober estimates lower these numbers to 580,000 and 54,000 respectively, but they remain impressive.[32] Against these insuperable odds, Hannibal brought a tiny army to Italy. We have an idea of its numbers from a tablet that he dedicated at the Temple of Juno Lacinia near Croton, just before he left Italy in 203. The inscription no longer exists, but Polybius thoughtfully copied it, telling us that Hannibal had only 20,000 infantry and 6,000 cavalry when he concluded his crossing of the Alps – half, Polybius says, of what he started with.[33] The accuracy of ancient numbers is always something of a guessing game, however, even when the person reporting them is as credible as Polybius. It is the degree of disparity between the two sides, rather than the actual numbers themselves, which is most useful in showing what Hannibal was up against.

This sort of glaring inequality had severely punished the most recent invader of Italy, Pyrrhus of Epirus, who had fought the Romans as the champion of the southern Italian city of Tarentum between 280 and 275. Pyrrhus was counting on a quick campaign, but became bogged down in a bloody war of attrition against a seemingly endless reservoir of Roman and Italian troops. After dramatically losing the opening engagements, the Romans finally got the better of Pyrrhus, who eventually admitted defeat and abandoned Tarentum to its fate. The Pyrrhic War was famous throughout the Mediterranean world, not least for giving Rome what Plutarch later called 'the reputation for invincibility'.[34] Hannibal could profit from its lessons; he was surely aware that the combined causes of Pyrrhus' defeat were the obstinacy of the Roman state and its huge supply of manpower. Hannibal's plan to succeed where Pyrrhus had failed was deceptively simple: inflict a crushing military defeat on Rome and shatter the myth of her invincibility. Such an event would inevitably cause Rome's allies to defect, and those desertions would swell Hannibal's ranks, evening the odds against Rome.[35] In support of this strategy was an ambitious programme of 'liberation propaganda', couched in the familiar language used by Hellenistic leaders to 'free' smaller states from larger ones.[36]

Before setting off for the Alps, Hannibal sacrificed at the Temple of Melqart at Gades in southern Spain. Melqart, a Phoenician deity, was equated with Hercules, whose myths and legends were widely known across the Mediterranean. One of Hercules' twelve labours had involved driving the oxen of Geryon from Spain to Greece in a route that passed over the Alps and through Italy. In the course of the journey, a giant named Cacus, who lived on the Aventine Hill (one of the seven hills of Rome), had attempted to steal the oxen; Hercules had killed him. The propaganda ploy was clear: Hannibal, whose itinerary into Italy mimicked the 'Herculean Way', was nothing less than a latter-day Hercules, a hero who would liberate those who suffered under the Roman yoke. It also mimicked Pyrrhus' earlier claim to be a liberator and played on Alexander the Great's connections with Hercules and other mythical heroes. The link, cemented from the very beginning through the sacrifice at Gades, gave Hannibal the 'divine aura' of the Hellenistic warrior-king and showed his troops – and those of his enemy – that he was favoured by the gods.[37]

Hannibal naturally hoped to convert this propaganda exercise into solid results, for not all of Rome's allies were enthusiastic about their 'friendship' with Rome. The Greek colonies of the south, such as Tarentum, had endured a particularly turbulent relationship with Rome. Furthermore, there were many Greek colonists in Sicily, which had been under Roman control since the end of the First Punic War. This unhappy situation was ripe for a new Hercules to slay the Roman giant.

Here, then, was Hannibal's tool to negate the very considerable advantages in Roman manpower. If he was to avoid the fate of Pyrrhus, he needed to capitalise on his guise as liberator, and to defeat Roman arms so thoroughly that Rome's allies would realise that they were better off joining his cause. As events would show, he came remarkably close to success.

As one of the more unconventional opening acts in military history, the crossing of the Alps is perhaps the most famous of Hannibal's exploits. This fame detracts from Hannibal's superb successes on the battlefield and also obscures the fact that his brother, Hasdrubal, carried out precisely the same journey later in the war – and in a shorter time. (Hasdrubal would be killed before he could get out of northern Italy, keeping his own trans-Alpine exploits firmly in the shadow of his brother.) Nevertheless, Livy was sufficiently impressed to write a grand tale about the journey, which still makes compelling reading.

The Alpine crossing, which followed a path out of Spain through what is now the South of France and over the mountains into Italy, took five months; it was probably completed sometime in the mid-autumn of 218. Preparations for the journey were meticulous. Hannibal found out everything he could about the terrain, food supplies and the people he would encounter. He used local guides and made every effort to safeguard his troops and animals.[38] Polybius says that he later went on a 'fact-finding tour in the Alps' to find out for himself what the journey had been like, but Hannibal's actual itinerary is still something of a mystery, and our understanding of it is reliant on the epic description given by Livy.[39] Hannibal's success resulted from his sheer determination and his ability to keep his troops going; even so, many soldiers, Livy says, dropped out of the march because they were more afraid of the crossing than of facing the Roman army on the other side.[40] Given Rome's fearsome reputation after beating both Pyrrhus and Carthage between 275 and 241, this observation tells us something about the difficulties of the journey.

A useful context for ancient descriptions of Hannibal's journey comes from Alexander the Great's war in Afghanistan. In 329, Alexander and his army crossed the mountains of the Hindu Kush in the face of heavy snow and food shortages. Even in the highlands which preceded the actual crossing, his troops suffered from snow-blindness and frost-bite; it was so cold that some who died on the ice became frozen to it, and their bodies had to be abandoned. Like Alexander, Hannibal and his men also faced the prospect of attacks from local inhabitants, and there was the ever-present risk of slipping into ravines and crevasses.[41] Hannibal found that his journey was particularly hard on the elephants, and he was constantly forced to come up with quick solutions for all sorts of problems. Early on, crossing the Rhône on the way to the Alps, Hannibal calmed his elephants at the river by using rafts with grass and earth, designed to look like dry land.[42] Later, in the mountains, he re-engineered part of the trail to negotiate a precipice, which delayed the army and its huge animals for four days – an impressive act for which Nepos praises him.[43] Polybius is clear that Hannibal lost nearly half of his invasion force in the crossing, saying that 'the constant suffering had reduced all the survivors to a state in which they resembled wild beasts'.[44]

While we may marvel at the tenacity that brought Hannibal and his army through this dangerous phase in the war, the real importance of the Alpine journey is the effect it had on Roman battle planning. When it became clear what Hannibal was up to, the Romans scrambled to revise their strategies: the Senate, together with the consuls for 218, Scipio the elder and Sempronius, had clearly envisaged a war fought in Spain and Africa, which would preserve Italy from invasion. But the Romans now realised that Hannibal was directly targeting Italy, and the Senate sent Scipio and his army to the mouth of the Rhône in an attempt to bring Hannibal to bay before he could reach the Alps. Despite a brief skirmish between Roman and Carthaginian solders, Hannibal eluded the main Roman effort and made his way into the Alpine foothills. Conceding the advantage to Hannibal, Scipio sent his army on to Spain under his brother Gnaeus, and then returned to northern Italy to take command of a fresh levy of troops. Sempronius, meanwhile, continued to Sicily, where optimistic preparations were still underway for an assault on Carthage.

Now in northern Italy, Hannibal rested his troops, restoring their health after their ordeal in the Alps. He then roused their zeal by allowing pairs of Gauls, captured during the Alpine crossing, to fight for their freedom. The choice for the combatants was literally life or death; far from home, Hannibal and his men needed either to crush the Romans or die trying. There was no middle ground.[45] The bloody metaphor resonated with the Carthaginian army and inspired Hannibal's soldiers to a quick victory over Scipio's untested army shortly afterwards at the Ticinus River in 218. Hannibal's soldiers were ready to fight and sure of their abilities. He had trained them personally, and together they had endured many years of shared combat in Spain as well as the long journey into Italy. In contrast, Scipio's army was a new levy, and he assumed command only for the one-year duration of his consulship. His militia buckled under the pressure of the Carthaginians' confidence, superiority in cavalry and – most of all – the respect and admiration they felt for their commander. The skirmish at the Ticinus was minor, but it had a devastating effect on Roman morale at a crucial time. Not only had Hannibal made it across the Alps, he had now beaten the Romans in battle. The action was still far from Rome, but another defeat might raise serious doubts about the safety of the city.

At the Ticinus, Scipio the elder was wounded. The younger Scipio, serving as a staff officer, is credited with saving his father's life.[46] The Romans abandoned the planned attack on Carthage and recalled Sempronius from Sicily. Both consuls, with a massed army, would face Hannibal at the River Trebia in December 218. In the three major engagements that followed – Trebia, Lake Trasimene and Cannae – Hannibal would demonstrate his understanding of his opponents, his appreciation of topography, the superiority of his cavalry and his use of deception in battle.[47]

In the run-up to the Trebia campaign, Hannibal's spies infiltrated the Roman camp and reported that there was tension between the consuls over the direction of the war. Hannibal knew that Sempronius was spoiling for a fight; there could be no greater glory for a Roman aristocrat than to crush an enemy on the battlefield, and the younger generation of Roman patricians yearned for the opportunities that their fathers and grandfathers had been given against Pyrrhus and then against Carthage in the First Punic War. Hannibal was here, in Italy. Rome itself was threatened, disaster just around the corner. Sempronius imagined himself the saviour of his country. Calls from Scipio, still wounded, pleading with his colleague to delay to rest and train the raw army, were drowned out by Sempronius' vision of his own glory. Given the choice, Hannibal preferred to fight the impetuous Sempronius rather than the more cautious Scipio. Knowing that the two consuls would have alternate days in supreme command, he made his plans accordingly.

By now the armies were camped close to one other, with the River Trebia between them. Determined to meet the Romans on his own terms, Hannibal reconnoitred a suitable location for the battle near the Roman position. He knew that the Romans could be aggressive and careless on open ground, and so the night before the battle he concealed his brother Mago with a picked force in a shallow depression to one side of the likely Roman advance.[48] On the day of the confrontation Hannibal's troops were well rested, fed and warmed by their campfires. A quick incursion against the Roman camp spurred Sempronius to action, and he ordered his troops to prepare for combat. Unlike their Carthaginian counterparts, the Romans, stumbling from their tents, had no time to fill their stomachs or light fires to ward off the winter cold. Sempronius then ordered them to ford the frigid Trebia in the December morning gloom to reach the Carthaginian lines.[49]

Despite these obstacles, the Roman effort began well enough: in the centre, the heavy infantry pushed their opponents back, bracing themselves against the sleet flying into their faces. But the tables quickly turned, as Hannibal's war elephants sparked a panic amongst the poorly trained Roman cavalry. Seeing the shock in the Roman formation when the cavalry fled, Mago sprung his trap, attacking the Roman flanks and the rear of their force. The victorious Roman centre had by now cut clean through their enemy. In an act of self-preservation, they retired from the battlefield as the rear ranks containing much of the army were encircled and massacred along the banks of the river.

Both consuls escaped, but the Trebia was another disaster for Roman morale. For Hannibal, the battle was a vindication of his detailed planning, intelligence-gathering apparatus, skill, relationship with his troops and his understanding of the weaknesses of his enemy. Inspecting the prisoners, Hannibal sent the Italians home, but threw the Roman citizens into irons. Given the disparity between the rights of Roman citizens and those of their Italian allies, many of whom possessed inferior grades of citizenship within the commonwealth, this was a clear message that spread quickly: Hannibal would liberate those whom Rome oppressed.

Hannibal had seized the initiative and now began to push for the decisive victory that would cause alliances to crumble and Rome to surrender. For the Romans, the debacle at the Trebia triggered a round of soul-searching, with grim results. Turning to the gods was a sure tactic in times of great crisis, but their answers after the Trebia only inspired greater terror. One of the new consuls, Flaminius, botched a sacrifice, causing the blood of a dying calf to be sprayed over the nearby onlookers, a menacing omen that filled those who witnessed it with despair.[50]

In early 217, Hannibal crossed the Apennines, seeing off a weak Roman challenge before heading towards Etruria (Tuscany). The Romans tried to keep Hannibal away from Rome by blocking the most likely routes south: Flaminius stationed himself at Arretium, and his colleague Servilius waited at Ariminum, on the Adriatic coast. Hannibal chose an extremely difficult route through the flood plain of the River Arno, which would bring him close to Arretium. There, he hoped to goad Flaminius into battle; he knew that Flaminius had won a reputation as reckless and cocksure, and so it would be to Hannibal's advantage to fight him, not Servilius, just as it had proved a good decision to oppose Sempronius, rather than Scipio.[51] This journey taxed his men to their limits. By now, all but one of Hannibal's elephants had died, and many of the horses had fallen ill. In the swamplands of the Arno, Hannibal's force suffered further from drowning and sleepless nights, while Hannibal himself caught an infection which may have blinded him in one eye.[52]

Emerging from the marshes, Hannibal harried and pillaged at will, determined to lure Flaminius away from the safety of Arretium's walls. Some of the Roman officers understood Hannibal's strategy and urged Flaminius to remain calm, but after a while the desire for action prevailed, and Flaminius marched out in hot pursuit of Hannibal's army. The hapless Roman general, though, was actually blundering to his death in one of the most famous traps in military history. Hannibal had once again chosen the battlefield: a narrow path by the shores of Lake Trasimene, where a thick, localised morning fog hung against the lake and along the base of the hills that looked on to it. In these hills, Hannibal had concealed most of his army, except for his rearguard, which he posted in full view of the Roman troops. The Romans struggled along the narrow path in preparation for an assault on what Flaminius assumed to be Hannibal's main force in front of them, but as they did so, they were suddenly attacked from the hills to their left. In the rear, a fresh contingent of Numidian (African) cavalry barred any hope of retreat. The Roman army was pinned against the lake, and now fought a frantic action in the fog while Flaminius tried to wrest control over his stricken column. The army disintegrated; some Roman legionaries fought courageous actions individually or in small groups, while others struggled into the lake, where they drowned under the weight of their armour or were killed by Hannibal's cavalry as it methodically searched the shallows, picking off the survivors. At some point, Flaminius and his bodyguards were killed in the fighting. Only a very small part of the army broke out of the trap, but was quickly captured, while a relief force of cavalry sent by Servilius was annihilated.[53] After the battle, Hannibal once again freed the Italian prisoners. He searched in vain for the body of Flaminius so that he could honour the fallen consul with burial.

The Romans responded to this disaster by appointing Quintus Fabius Maximus as 'dictator'; this was an emergency six-month position used only in periods of great crisis. Fabius would avoid battle with Hannibal, earning the unflattering nickname 'The Delayer' from those who misinterpreted his actions as cowardice. Hannibal admired Fabius as an intelligent and thoughtful general and, finding that Fabius could not easily be drawn into a confrontation, sought other ways to maintain his own advantage. He knew that Fabius was facing a mounting chorus of dissent towards his policy, and so he pillaged the area around Fabius' estates, but left the estates themselves alone, prompting uncomfortable questions for Fabius in the Roman Senate about his 'arrangement' with the Carthaginian commander. In one of his most famous deceptions, Hannibal escaped a night-time trap that Fabius had laid for him by attaching firebrands to the horns of a herd of oxen, which he drove along, creating the illusion of an army on the move while he escaped in the opposite direction.[54] Fabius' enemies seized on this failure, and the young and arrogant Minucius, Fabius' second in command, engineered a promotion for himself as co-dictator. The position had no constitutional precedent and reveals a certain desperation in Rome for decisive action.

Against Fabius, though, Hannibal was unable to win the dramatic victory which he desired; he felt further frustration when his requests for reinforcements were repeatedly turned down in Carthage.[55] Eventually this uneasy period came to a close with the automatic expiration of Fabius' position. New consular elections were held: the incumbents for 216 were Aemilius Paullus, a man of military experience and great integrity, and Varro, a demagogue disparaged by Livy for his left-wing tendencies. Once again, Hannibal knew which commander he would prefer to fight.

Hannibal's great victory at Cannae in 216 earned a hallowed place in the pantheon of Roman defeats: over half a millennium later, it was still a byword for catastrophe. Writing about the death of the Emperor Valens and the slaughter of the Roman army at Adrianople (AD 378), the Roman officer and historian Ammianus Marcellinus lamented that 'in the annals there is no record of such a massacre, other than the one at Cannae'.[56]

The Roman defeat in 216 was the result of a number of factors, including popular resentment towards the tactics of Fabius, the humiliation of the preceding years, the burning ambition of Roman commanders and the rivalry between Varro and Paullus. Hannibal knew that Paullus would approach him cautiously, and so he determined instead to turn Varro's carelessness and aggression against him. The army assembled by the Romans was colossal, double the normal levy for each of the two consuls. Combined, it may have numbered close to 80,000 men – an instrument designed to bludgeon its way to victory.

Hannibal, though, had learned a great deal from fighting the Romans. Their army was grouped around company-sized tactical units called maniples. While the development of the maniple had given the Roman army greater flexibility, these formations were still unable to wheel or flank effectively on the battlefield. Instead, as they had shown at the Trebia, they were extremely strong in the advance, but unable to respond to an encircling manoeuvre or initiate one themselves. These limitations would eventually be overcome by Scipio Africanus, but the army assembled to fight Hannibal in 216 still privileged an aggressive frontal attack over innovation and flexibility. Compounding this problem was the fact that, due to the casualties of previous years, much of the army was raw and untested.

The Romans and Carthaginians camped close to the village of Cannae in the heat of the summer of 216. Paullus, Livy says, argued caution, but Varro, like Sempronius, would hear none of it. In his camp, Hannibal was encouraged by this news from his spies: he was eager to face Varro, for whom he designed a famous and deadly trap. On a day when Varro was in command, Hannibal offered battle, arranging his weakest forces in a bow formation whose centre bulged outwards towards the Roman lines. (According to Appian, Hannibal also concealed cavalry in nearby ravines and placed part of his force to take advantage of a powerful wind that would blow in the faces of his opponents.[57]) On the wings, he stationed his veteran infantry and his cavalry. The Roman attack was assertive and belligerent. It drove the Carthaginian centre back, and the strong advance of the Roman maniples steadily turned the convex bow into a concave depression, which deepened as Varro began to sense that success was imminent and Roman momentum accelerated. On the wings, however, obscured from the vantage point of Varro and his officers by the dust kicked up by thousands of men and horses, the superior Numidian cavalry chased its weak Roman counterpart from the field. This deprived the legions of their only hope of protection against a flanking manoeuvre. Meanwhile, the concave bow had now turned into a deepening 'U' shape, with the Romans increasingly penned in by the three sides of the 'U'. Consternation, and then panic, spread throughout the Roman infantry as they realised their predicament; now, Hannibal's veterans, stationed on the flanks of the 'U' and no longer concerned about the Roman horsemen, turned inward and attacked the Romans from the sides.

The discipline and cohesion of the maniples – superior in the advance, but unable to wheel to face this new threat – crumbled as the battle broke down, as at Lake Trasimene, into a series of individual and group combats as desperate legionaries tried to break free. Further problems were caused by the earlier 'surrender' of 500 Spanish mercenaries, who now attacked the Romans from the rear, where they had been sequestered – another pre-planned deception by Hannibal.[58] Worse followed when Hannibal's cavalry, fresh from routing the Roman horsemen, returned to the fight and helped the infantry complete a double envelopment of the doomed Roman army.

By the afternoon, almost all of the Roman soldiers lay dead. Among the casualties was the consul Paullus; dead, too, were scores of senators who had volunteered for the ranks in the battle that was supposed to end the war, and lying alongside them in the blood-soaked dust lay a host of notable individuals, including Minucius and Servilius, the consul of 217. Varro somehow escaped with a small contingent to the village of Venusia. Astonishingly, he eventually returned to Rome, where he was praised for not giving up on the state in its darkest hour; Livy notes sourly that a Carthaginian general in his position would have been crucified.[59] Some soldiers sought refuge in the two camps that the Roman consuls had established before the battle but were soon taken prisoner.

Another group made its way to the town of Canusium, one of whose number was a young staff officer, Scipio the younger.[60] Some of the patricians amongst the group declared that all was lost and urged those around them to flee Italy. Scipio responded to this defeatist talk by drawing his sword and holding it dramatically above his head. He swore allegiance to Rome in front of Jupiter Optimus Maximus, the king of the gods, and called on those around him to steady themselves and pledge their loyalty and their commitment to victory.[61] In the aftermath of Rome's greatest military defeat, the revival – at least for Livy – was already underway.

3

The Fate of Pyrrhus

He often looked back at the shores of Italy.

Livy, 30.20

In the aftermath of his victory at Cannae, Hannibal's lieutenant Marhabal is said to have advised his master to attack Rome and finish the war, but Hannibal did nothing.[62] Livy says that this moment saved the Republic, but the reality is not as clear-cut; the anecdote itself, in any case, may have originally been associated with the aftermath of Trasimene, before the even greater triumph at Cannae prompted storytellers to embellish the tale.[63] Could the war really have ended in 216, if Hannibal had attacked and captured Rome? Livy imagines Hannibal thinking obsessively about his failure to do so as he sailed from Italy for the final confrontation in Africa.[64] Yet it may not even have been necessary to capture the city; approaching it in force, or blockading it, might have been sufficient to underscore Roman weakness for the benefit of undecided allies.[65] Later in the war Hannibal did indeed march on Rome to alleviate pressure on his ally Capua, causing panic in the city and diverting a large Roman force from its own operations, although his foray eventually came to nothing.[66]

It seems clear, however, that capturing or destroying Rome was never a Carthaginian war aim.[67] In a speech to Roman prisoners after Cannae, Hannibal declared that his fight was not to the death, but only for 'honour and empire'.[68] The treaty that Hannibal would later make with King Philip V of Macedon shows that both men imagined that Rome would still exist following a Carthaginian victory. Hannibal probably expected that the series of stunning blows he had delivered at Trebia, Trasimene and Cannae would bring the enemy to the bargaining table, leaving him victorious.[69] In other words, Hannibal would fight only as long as necessary for the Romans to admit that they were beaten, and agree to terms that would reduce their footprint in Italy and restore to Carthage (at a bare minimum) what had been lost to Rome in the first war. 'Honour and empire' would be satisfied.[70] In this strategy he could take some inspiration from Pyrrhus, who, albeit eventually overwhelmed by Roman resilience and determination, *had* succeeded in attracting many of the southern Italian communities to his cause, *had* beaten the Roman army repeatedly and *had* brought the Senate to the negotiating table. Pyrrhus' embassy was rebuffed, to be sure, but only just.[71] Had not Hannibal achieved much of this by 216? He had even tried negotiations, although his envoy, Carthalo, had been sent packing.[72]

The cracks that appeared in Rome's network of alliances from 216 suggest that Hannibal was indeed having an impact. Livy provides a catalogue of peoples and cities that defected to Hannibal as they nervously digested the scale of Roman defeats.[73] In that list were some of the usual suspects who had chafed under Roman rule: Tarentum, for example, as well as the Samnites. Southern Italy, still restive in the aftermath of the Pyrrhic wars, had a large number of defections. No Latin city (from Latium, the region around Rome) defected, but in 209, twelve Latin colonies declared themselves unable to provide men for the war, revealing the degree of pressure that Hannibal's campaign was inflicting on the alliance network.

Polybius says that it was extraordinary that Hannibal was able to beat the Romans so decisively in battle and come so close to total success.[74] Yet in the end, and despite all his efforts to avoid it, Hannibal shared the fate of Pyrrhus: sunk by the immense strength of the Republic. Why was this? Partly, it was because the desertions from Rome would never be enough, and those that did stray needed Hannibal's protection from Roman reprisals, something that his small force could never guarantee. In some defected towns, pro-Roman politicians sometimes succeeded in forcing a reversal of allegiance, while elsewhere, Hannibal's poor diplomacy, in glaring contrast to that of the younger Scipio in Spain, produced equally poor results.[75]

Hannibal had also misunderstood his opponent, a terrible irony for one with a gift of reading the intentions of Roman commanders. As the Senate and the Roman people had survived Pyrrhus, they would survive Hannibal, no matter how long the fight. Indeed, read in retrospect, Plutarch's verdict on Pyrrhus is eye-opening. Pyrrhus, Plutarch wrote:

> had lost a great part of the forces with which he came, and all his friends and generals except a few; moreover, he had no others whom he could summon from home, and he saw that his allies in Italy were

becoming indifferent, while the army of the Romans, as if from a fountain gushing forth indoors, was easily and speedily filled up again, and they did not lose courage in defeat – nay, their wrath gave them all the more vigour and determination for the war.[76]

The Romans confounded all expectations by fighting on after Cannae, engaging in a 'total war' of the sort that Hannibal and the military tradition of the Hellenistic world could not completely understand.[77] States were expected to negotiate after crushing defeats like Trasimene or Cannae – but the Romans did the exact opposite. Unmistakable signals of senatorial intent can be found in the recruitment of legions of slaves, the young and the indebted, as well as in the assigning of survivors of Cannae into punishment brigades to serve out the war in Sicily (Scipio would later restore their honour at Zama). The decision to leave Rome alone was not the cause of Hannibal's eventual defeat. Rather, the impressive resilience of Rome's political will, the stubbornness of the majority of Rome's allies, Rome's ability to find yet more troops and to arm them for war, and of course the rise of Scipio, all played a role in guiding Hannibal inexorably towards defeat.

Following the victory at Cannae, Hannibal sent his brother Mago to deliver a report on their success to the Carthaginian Senate and to obtain reinforcements. Mago's bulletin was met with delight and rejoicing, but resentment against Hannibal was still to be found in the person of Hanno, clinging on as leader of the anti-Barcid faction. Livy imagines Hanno arguing for an end to the war, saying that Carthage should grant peace before it was too late.[78] Nevertheless, the Barcids won the day: Mago poured a torrent of gold rings taken from dead Roman aristocrats on to the floor, and troops were raised. A small force was ordered to sail for Italy – in the end, the only real effort ever made by Carthage to help Hannibal – while the Senate also allowed a larger complement of mercenaries to be raised in Spain.[79]

Meanwhile, Hannibal focused much of his attention in 216 on Campania. He was keen to win over Naples, since a port would greatly strengthen his communications with Carthage and facilitate the movement of supplies and reinforcements, but his army was not adequate for the task of capturing such a well-defended target. As Hannibal moved from place to place in search of defections and quick conquests, the Roman commander Marcellus shadowed him from his base at Casilinum. Hannibal did have some success at Nuceria, where he starved the town into submission, and then sacked and burned it; elsewhere, Hannibal continued efforts to exploit divisions between Romans and Italians, offering to reward Italians if they joined his cause.[80] Marcellus watched anxiously. His apprehension was justified, since Hannibal had earlier achieved a spectacular success in his effort to prise apart Rome's alliance network.

In 216, the important Campanian city of Capua defected from Rome. The climate of resentment in the city towards its over-dominant patron to the north was already febrile, and a slight prod pushed the city to an open revolt. Control of Capua and the territory it encompassed, which included numerous ports, promised Hannibal one thing he greatly needed and had failed to achieve at Naples: a link to the sea.[81] Hannibal made a favourable treaty with Capua. No Campanian citizen would have to serve in the army against his will; Capua would retain its ancient laws and customs free from Carthaginian interference and would gain back land confiscated by Rome. Rejoicing at their fortune, the Capuans reinforced their shift in loyalty by suffocating a group of Roman citizens and military officers in the public bathhouse.[82] In a speech to the Capuan Senate, Hannibal promised that Capua would be the main city of Italy, a stunning reversal from Capua's previous position as a Roman client.[83] Adding to Carthaginian fortunes, a further success came at Casilinum. With Marcellus absent from the town, Hannibal blockaded and finally captured it. The siege caused such privation that the garrison resorted to eating the leather from their own shields, along with mice and roots. Casilinum was handed over to Capua to administer.[84]

Hannibal and his army made Capua their base for the winter of 216/15. Appian and Livy claim that discipline in the Carthaginian army collapsed during this period as the men, exhausted and brutalised after more than three years of savage and relentless campaigning, gave themselves over to the city's vices.[85] Interestingly, Appian's comments about poor behaviour are specifically directed at Hannibal himself, casting a singular (albeit Roman) piece of doubt over portraits of his chastity and restraint.

Livy even has Marcellus say that the sojourn at Capua was 'Hannibal's Cannae'.[86]

The year 215 brought mixed fortunes for Hannibal. He learned that his brother Hasdrubal had been held at bay by Roman forces under the elder Scipios near the River Ebro. The Roman victory triggered a cascade of defections from Hasdrubal's Spanish allies. On the other hand, the army won from the Carthaginian Senate by Mago landed in southern Italy under the command of an officer named Bomilcar, while Mago himself was sent to Spain. The young and ambitious tyrant of Syracuse, Hieronymus, who had succeeded his staunchly pro-Roman grandfather Hiero, weighed his options and made overtures towards Hannibal. Syracuse was the most powerful of the Sicilian cities, and an alliance with Carthage, through which Syracuse might extend its sway over all of Sicily, represented an ominous threat to Roman interests. Hieronymus was murdered in 214, but eastern Sicily remained riven by factional politics that drew Rome into a long struggle. Further afield, Hannibal also agreed to a treaty of mutual assistance with the Macedonian monarch Philip V, who, like Hieronymus, nursed designs to extend his power.[87]

The treaty with Philip did not really help Hannibal, although a Macedonian contingent fought at Zama in 202. However, once the Romans learned of the treaty, they launched a campaign to prevent Philip from keeping his side of the bargain. The resulting naval patrols in the Adriatic, and a land campaign in Greece – fought largely by anti-Macedonian proxies with Roman assistance –

focused the king's attention closer to home.[88] The fact that Rome could open a new front so soon after Cannae illustrates the Republic's astonishing determination, but more importantly, this part of the war set a precedent for Roman interference in Greek affairs and contributed to Rome's eventual conquest of the eastern Mediterranean. While the so-called First Macedonian War concluded in 205, the Romans delivered an ultimatum to Philip in the aftermath of Zama and were at war with him again in 200. Hannibal's treaty, although doing little for his war effort, widened the scope of the conflict and fixed Rome's predatory gaze on the east, with significant long-term consequences.

Meanwhile, the Carthaginians continued to push for gains in southern Italy. In 214, Hanno (not the anti-Barcid politician, but Hannibal's nephew), campaigned in Bruttium. The city of Locri, after allowing the Roman garrison to escape, offered its friendship to the Carthaginians, but this was one of the few successes. In 214, Hanno was recalled northwards, only to be defeated at Beneventum, where the Romans had beaten Pyrrhus just over sixty years earlier. Hannibal then moved into Apulia, leaving his Campanian allies undefended. Casilinum was recaptured by Marcellus, who had now been elected consul alongside the former dictator Fabius. The Romans had begun to rebuild their strength: Marcellus went on to mastermind the capture of Syracuse in 212, ending a campaign famous for the involvement of the mathematician Archimedes, whose 'super-weapons' were said to have done much to frustrate the Roman assault.

In the same year Hannibal did succeed in capturing part of Tarentum, along with a number of other towns in southern Italy, but these successes would be short lived.

In 211/10, a vengeful Roman force made a concerted effort on Capua. Hannibal marched towards Rome to alleviate pressure on the Capuan defenders, and as the people of Rome panicked, a Roman detachment was seconded from siege duties at Capua to bar the way. Hannibal stopped at the Temple of Hercules outside the city walls, perhaps hoping to reinforce his heroic persona, but in the end, nothing happened. Fulvius Flaccus, the Roman commander, was keen to engage Hannibal, but thunderstorms prevented the two sides from meeting. Livy delights in the story that while Hannibal was frustrated outside the walls, a Roman force set out for the war in Spain from the other side of the city. In an even more glaring piece of Roman propaganda, Livy states that the land that Hannibal was camped on was sold for its full market value, even while the Carthaginians remained close to the Roman defences.[89]

Hannibal abandoned Capua to its fate. The buildings were spared, but the population was killed, deported or sold. Hannibal then lost allies in Samnium as he withdrew to the south. If news reached him from Spain that his brother Mago and Hasdrubal (son of Gisgo) had defeated and killed the elder Scipios, it may not greatly have cheered him. Bad news from Sicily in 210 and then the final loss of Tarentum in 209 were further blows. The victor at Tarentum, Fabius Maximus, had taken the city by a fifth column after luring Hannibal away. The story, as told by Plutarch, features a weary Hannibal giving Fabius his grudging respect.[90]

With Capua, the Samnites and Tarentum lost, Hannibal was penned into Bruttium. In 208 he enjoyed a rare success at Venusia, not far from Cannae, where he ambushed and killed an uncharacteristically impetuous Marcellus and the consul Crispinus. Hannibal paid tribute to Marcellus, saying that while he looked up to Fabius as a teacher, he respected Marcellus as an opponent.[91] This was high praise from Hannibal, who sought out the body of Marcellus for burial. Always alert to an opportunity to steal a tactical advantage, however, Hannibal then took the fallen consul's signet ring and used it to create a fraudulent order, in a vain attempt to get the citizens of nearby Salapia to open their city to him. It was a fine example, for later writers, of 'Punic perfidy'.[92]

Finally, in 207, Hannibal received a lifeline. His brother Hasdrubal had broken out of Spain and crossed over the Alps into Italy. By the spring, Hasdrubal was in the Po Valley.[93] A nightmare scenario of a double-strength Carthaginian force was in place for the Romans, but what followed was, incredibly, a remarkable Roman triumph. A message from Hasdrubal to his brother, proposing that the two Carthaginian armies meet in Umbria, was intercepted. Rapid preparations were made by the two consuls, Claudius Nero and Livius Salinator, to face the threat. While Livius was assigned to deal with Hasdrubal, Nero kept a close watch on Hannibal's camp in the south. But, with a spontaneity uncharacteristic of Roman commanders in the war, Nero made to link up with Livius and slipped out of his camp with a picked force, sending messengers ahead to order the towns and villages on his route to stand by with food, drink and fresh horses. A blistering forced march followed, while the remainder of Nero's army remained close to the Carthaginian camp to hold Hannibal in place. In the north, the two consuls billeted their men together to give the appearance of a single army, and the combined force caught up with the Carthaginians at the Metaurus River. Hasdrubal was killed in a rout that Appian memorably described as divine compensation for the massacre at Cannae.[94] Nero delivered Hasdrubal's severed head to Hannibal, while two freed African prisoners told their general what had happened. Hannibal, it is said, then recognised that his fate was sealed.[95]

By 206/5, Carthaginian resistance in Spain had collapsed, and a desperate attempt by Carthage to reinforce the Italian situation under Hannibal's brother Mago proved inconclusive. It was at this point that Hannibal had the inscription detailing the strength of his force engraved at the Temple of Juno Lacinia near Croton, as a testament to his endeavours. He had achieved much with the tiny force that he had brought into Italy, yet he was vastly outnumbered by his enemy and never fully understood, it seems, the strength and tenacity of the people he was facing. His propaganda campaign, directed towards Rome's allies, had never succeeded at the level required to guarantee victory. Following the defeat of Mago in 204, with no meaningful assistance from Philip V, and then with the Romans preparing the invasion of

Africa, it became clear that the game was up. In 203, with Roman forces testing Carthaginian resolve in Africa itself, Hannibal was finally recalled to face his most famous opponent: Scipio Africanus.

4

Scipio and the Roman Revival

Almost the most famous man of all time.

Polybius, 10.2, on Scipio

The resolve of the Senate and the Roman generals stands out as a decisive factor in the revival of Roman fortunes in the Hannibalic War. The vagaries of history have, however, turned the younger Scipio into the main cause of Hannibal's defeat. Scipio is best known for the Battle at Zama in 202, but if we are to understand the importance of his contribution to the war effort, then we must focus on Spain. It was in Spain that he proved his brilliance, and it was there that he forged an improved Roman army that was the equal of the Carthaginian veterans. Spain was crucial to the Roman victory.[96]

Scipio occupies a much smaller place in the overall narrative of the war, because he was only a very young man when the conflict started, and at that time other members of his family, the Scipiones branch of the Cornelii, held prominent positions in the Roman hierarchy. We know rather little about his early life. Polybius states that Scipio was 17 at the time of the contest at the Ticinus River, placing his birth sometime in 236/5. His father was Publius Cornelius, the consul for 218; his mother was Pomponia. At some point he married Aemilia, the daughter of Aemilius Paullus (consul 216); the Cornelii and Aemilii were long-time political allies. At the Ticinus he is credited with saving his father's life with a selfless solo charge against the Carthaginian cavalry; this act gave the young Scipio an early and widespread reputation for courage.[97]

Nothing further is heard of Scipio until the disaster at Cannae, where he rallied the band of survivors. Four years later, Scipio was elected as curule aedile, a junior magistracy on the Roman career ladder. In a society that placed a premium on the wisdom of its elders, age, experience and previous service were usually prerequisites for appointment to office; since Scipio was well below the qualifying age, his election was controversial. Livy says that Scipio did not debate the constitutional technicalities but simply deferred to the will of the people, who then promptly acclaimed him on the strength of his early war record and his family name.[98] Scipio's seemingly innocuous decision to let the people decide, while casting him as a willing public servant, also represented something of an individualistic challenge to the customs of the state: it was the elders in the Senate, not the people, who determined policy. In hindsight, it was an ominous portent of things to come.

Scipio served his aedileship without incident. Shortly afterwards, in 211, he found himself head of the family due to the deaths of his father and his uncle in combat. Both Publius and Gnaeus had enjoyed success in the Spanish campaign, an aspect of the war often overshadowed by the dramatic events in Italy and the showdown in Africa. Nevertheless, from the very beginning Spain had been a vital part of Roman strategy. A Roman army had been stationed there since the very beginning of the war, and the elder Scipios had won a notable victory over Hannibal's brother Hasdrubal in 215. By 212, Saguntum had been captured and became the base of Roman operations.

The following year, confident and rashly dividing their forces, both Scipio brothers were killed within a short time of each other. Total disaster was averted by a Roman officer, Marcius, who rallied the scattered remnants of the army. After a brief interlude under the future consul Claudius Nero, the Senate opened up the Spanish command for competition. It would carry the rank of proconsul, which meant that the incumbent would have the *imperium* (legal authority) of a consul but was not one of the two regular elected consular officials. Proconsuls were drawn from a limited group whose members usually had prior service as consuls and extensive experience in government. Rather surprisingly, none of the expected candidates from this group submitted his name on election day. Livy says that this was due to widespread rumours about how dire the situation had become in Spain.[99] Whether or not this was true, it has the convenient literary effect of highlighting the courage and audacity of the only man who did, finally, step forward and offer his candidacy: Scipio.

Just as Scipio had been too young to be aedile, he was also, at 24, far too young and inexperienced to hold proconsular *imperium*. Nevertheless, the crowd roared their approval as he stepped forward, only to turn anxious when they realised quite how inexperienced he really was.[100] What happened next, if true as Livy recounts it, says a great deal about Scipio, and the fame and influence of his family. Keenly aware of the problem surrounding his age, he revived the crowd's enthusiasm, making them confident that the Roman forces would be victorious under his guidance. How had he persuaded them?

Scipio possessed an innate empathic ability to sense the mood of the people and to guide them in whichever direction he chose. This gift would prove invaluable in Spain, where he waged a diplomatic charm offensive on Carthage's Spanish allies. Livy implies that this was not a mere gift of oratory, for elsewhere he derides Roman politicians who had a talent for demagoguery and speeches.[101] Instead, he suggests that Scipio's ability to charm the people was based on the deliberate and public cultivation of divine favour.[102] Scipio, Livy says, was accustomed to concluding his daily affairs only after he had spent a considerable amount of time alone in the Temple of Jupiter on the Capitoline Hill. Both Livy and Polybius are clear that such acts were politically motivated and the product of a calculating mind.[103] In addition to allowing rumours to develop that he was able to commune with the gods, Scipio also varied the way he acted to match the feelings of the people, who became accustomed to seeing the hand of divine support in his successes.[104] In the highly religious world of the ancient Mediterranean, and with the precedent of Alexander and his successors claiming links with – or even descent from – the divine, the idea that Scipio could be similarly well connected was credible, especially during a time of great desperation and uncertainty. Interestingly, the mystique that Scipio cultivated was not at all dissimilar to that which cloaked Hannibal as a semi-divine avatar of Hercules. Later on,

Scipio would also become associated with Hercules, in a literary battle over who truly had heavenly support during the war.

Combined with the reputation of the Cornelii Scipiones, public sympathy for the loss of his father and uncle, and the search for a saviour, the apparently privileged relationship that Scipio held with heaven was enough for the people to assign him, as a private citizen invested with proconsular *imperium*, to the Spanish command.

In 210, according to Livy, the war hung in the balance. The Romans had recaptured Capua but lost Tarentum; the Carthaginians had beaten the Scipio brothers in Spain but not pressed their attack further; Hannibal had stared at the walls of Rome, but nothing had come of it.[105] Fortune, though, would rapidly turn against Carthage. Hannibal was increasingly confined to southern Italy and could only watch in dismay as, in just five short years, Scipio trained a new Roman army and systematically dismantled the generals that Carthage had stationed in Spain.

This campaign began in the autumn of 210. As a rumour spread throughout the Roman armies in Spain that he had been sent by the gods to end the war, Scipio gathered his forces at the mouth of the River Ebro.[106] He thanked them for their loyalty to his father and uncle and praised their performance and that of their commander, Marcius, who had saved them when all seemed lost. In all of this he deliberately played upon his own physical resemblance to his father, and the bond between the veterans of the

Spanish campaign and the Scipio family.[107] The young Roman general was, consciously or not, doing much the same as Hannibal, evoking the powerful ties wrought by years of shared privation, victories and challenges. Scipio presented himself as part of an unbroken chain of generalship that stretched back to the first landing in Spain of Gnaeus and his troops in 218. Like Hannibal, he also promoted, or at least did little to deter, the growth of a divine mystique around his actions.[108]

Three Carthaginian armies were stationed in Spain under the command of Hasdrubal and Mago, the brothers of Hannibal, and Hasdrubal (son of Gisgo). They outnumbered the Romans, and Scipio felt that an attack on any one of the armies might leave him stranded, or worse, fighting all three simultaneously. Instead, knowing that the three armies were hundreds of miles away, he decided to ignore them for the moment and strike unexpectedly at the centre of Carthaginian power in Spain: New Carthage. The city, deep in enemy territory, was built on a peninsula that jutted into the sea, guarded on its west and north sides by a lagoon of variable depth; a narrow strip of land connected the peninsula to the mainland and created a natural bottleneck for any infantry assault. However, while it looked formidable, it was only defended by a tiny garrison. It was also a highly enticing target. It was Carthage's major Spanish port and had a valuable repository of weapons, cash and the political hostages drawn from the Spanish tribes that were imprisoned there. Freeing those hostages was a precious propaganda opportunity that could not be missed. Confiding his plan only to his lieutenant, Laelius, Scipio ordered the fleet and his army south.

The assault itself was based on an elaborate deception, and its ultimate success seemed to be ordained by the gods themselves. While a costly escalade was attempted on the walls of the city and naval artillery pounded the battlements, Scipio led a picked force through the lagoon. With the defenders of New Carthage concentrating on the assault from land and sea, the part of the city facing the lagoon was undefended. Scipio had learned from fishermen that at certain times the breeze and tide combined to create a shallow, fordable path through the lagoon, but he concealed the origin of this intelligence and instead circulated the rumour that Neptune had appeared to him in a dream and shown him the way.[109] Quickly over the walls and into the city, the Roman assault force opened the gates of the town, and the commander of the garrison soon surrendered. The plunder was immense and included ships, food, timber, gold, silver and siege equipment, all of which passed into Scipio's purse.[110] Of greater value was the group of Spanish hostages that he captured. He restored them to their families and appointed an officer to return their property. Livy uses a story of a young female hostage to illustrate Scipio's magnanimity. Rather than claim the young girl as a spoil of war, he instead reunited her with her fiancé, loaded them both with presents and sent them on their way, asking only for friendship in return. This story, and others like it, inspired numerous paintings entitled *The Continence of Scipio* by artists such as di Giovanni (1463/5), Poussin (1640) and Allan (1774).

Scipio had won a stunning and unexpected military victory, but with his treatment of the captured hostages, he also accomplished a feat of propaganda, the importance of which Hannibal had been quite unable to match in Italy. Laelius sailed to Rome to announce the victory to the Senate, while Scipio drilled his soldiers relentlessly to maintain their physical condition and morale. Meanwhile, the three Carthaginian generals suppressed news of the defeat, putting out instead that Scipio was young and arrogant and was carried away by the trivial capture of an inconsequential target.[111] In reality, however, they were watching nervously, since they knew how serious their predicament had suddenly become.

During the winter of 209/8, Scipio allowed the gravity of his victory to impress itself on Carthage's Spanish allies. Edeco, a prominent nobleman, went to see Scipio at Tarraco, and Mandonius and Indibilis, very much the most powerful men in Spain, went over to Rome.[112] Emboldened, Scipio prepared to attack Hasdrubal (Hannibal's brother) before he could link up with the other two Carthaginian armies. Scipio refitted his army with weapons taken from New Carthage and, in command of the coast, enrolled his marines into the legions. He then embarked on an innovative training programme for his troops, designed to enable the maniples in his army to form rapidly into larger units (cohorts) at a single command. The ability to switch easily from maniples to cohorts and vice versa gave the army greater options for density, flexibility and manoeuvre than in the past. These attributes would be key factors in Scipio's success in the remainder of the Spanish campaign, where cohorts were used to hammer the enemy flanks, an elasticity quite unthinkable for many of Scipio's contemporaries.[113] With this augmented, well-trained and re-equipped force, he set out to find Hasdrubal in the summer of 208.

Contact was made near Baecula, where the Roman vanguard met Hasdrubal's cavalry pickets. Scipio's light infantry went efficiently and confidently into the attack, reflecting the high level of morale in the Roman force.[114] After this brief skirmish, Hasdrubal moved his camp to a hill, well protected by steep sides and backed by a river. A plateau at the top afforded the Carthaginian general plenty of room and looked down on to a sloping plain, where he posted his light-armed troops and cavalry. Confident of his strong position, he awaited Scipio's offer of battle.

The Roman assault at Baecula is a good example of the type of tactical thinking, pioneered by Scipio, which was a decisive break from the blunt one-dimensional frontal attack that had characterised the Roman approach at the Trebia and at Cannae.[115] First, Scipio led a large force against the Carthaginian light-armed troops and cavalry that protected the approaches to Hasdrubal's position, pushing them back under heavy fire. In possession of the lower slope, Scipio ordered Laelius around one side of the hill, while he took another part of the force in the opposite direction. The remainder of the army continued its advance, fixing the attention of much of Hasdrubal's army while Scipio and Laelius flanked it from both sides, climbing the steep slope in a disciplined formation.

Faced with attack from three directions, the Carthaginian lines collapsed, the elephants in the army panicked, and Hasdrubal fled. Oddly, Scipio did not pursue him, allowing him to go on to cross the Alps and invade Italy. Hundreds of the enemy were captured, and as he had done at New Carthage, Scipio showed clemency towards Spaniards, mirroring once again Hannibal's approach to the Italians. One particular prisoner offered the opportunity for a major diplomatic breakthrough: a young boy who turned out to be the grandson of a Numidian king, Masinissa, one of the most formidable of the Carthaginian allies and a key figure in the defeat of Scipio's father. Scipio presented the youngster with gifts and sent him with a Roman escort to be reunited with Masinissa, who was still in Spain. This display of clemency would have momentous repercussions.[116]

The fallout from Scipio's victory was significant. The three Carthaginian commanders were forced to acknowledge the damaging effect that Scipio's gracious approach to the Spanish tribes was having on their own efforts to retain their loyalty. They decided that drastic action was needed to tip the balance of the war back in Carthage's favour: Hasdrubal would have to go to Italy to help Hannibal (as we have seen, he was killed there at the Metaurus in 207); Mago went to the Balearic Islands to raise troops; Masinissa would harass Scipio's supply lines; and Hasdrubal (son of Gisgo) would, for the time being, avoid direct confrontation with the main Roman force.[117] Meanwhile, Scipio was unexpectedly hailed as king by the Spaniards, a title which was anathema to his Republican loyalties. He told them to call him not *rex*, but *imperator*, the title that had fallen into favour among his troops. This label is better known from the late Republic, where it was used by the legions almost as a form of adoration to salute victorious commanders such as Julius Caesar. This appears to be its first recorded use and reflects the close relationship developing between Scipio and his soldiers.[118]

By 207/6, eastern Spain was largely under Roman control. Hasdrubal (son of Gisgo – henceforth, just Hasdrubal) was at Gades, while further reinforcements had reached Mago. Characteristically, Scipio determined to strike before the different groups could be combined into a single formidable opponent. His lieutenant Silanus drove Mago to flight; only a tiny portion of the Carthaginian force survived to reach Hasdrubal, who then withdrew into the countryside in southern Spain and quartered his army in its towns and villages. Scipio assigned his brother Lucius to attack Orongis, the most powerful of the towns in the area, in a demonstration of Roman strength. Livy praises the discipline of the Roman force, noting that no unarmed civilians were killed, although he glosses over the unfortunate deaths of several hundred townspeople who, trying to escape the impending conflagration, ran out of the gates of Orongis and were cut down by Roman soldiers before they realised their mistake.[119]

While Hasdrubal recovered from his losses, Scipio and his troops passed the winter of 207/6 at Tarraco. In the spring, Hasdrubal and Mago raised a large army and congregated around the town of Ilipa. Scipio marched to meet them, hiring an additional force of Spanish mercenaries. After some desultory clashes, the two sides engaged each other.

Ilipa is one of Scipio's most celebrated victories. It was achieved against a much larger force and made strong use of deception and innovative thinking. For several days, Scipio and Hasdrubal drew up their troops for battle. Each day Scipio placed his best troops, his Roman legionaries, in the centre, with his weakest, the Spanish allies, on the wings. Opposing the legions in the Carthaginian centre were Hasdrubal's African veterans. When neither side accepted battle, both retired, and this charade continued for several days. Then, on the third evening, Scipio ordered his troops and animals to receive extra rest and food, and the following morning, in the pre-dawn mists, he formed up for battle. Hasdrubal was taken completely by surprise as he stared out at Scipio's formation, which had now reversed itself. The best troops were on the wings, the weakest in the centre. Alarmed at this turn of events, the Carthaginians stumbled from their tents and prepared to receive the impending Roman assault.[120]

For a while, Scipio kept his troops in relaxed formation as his skirmishers and cavalry wore away at the tired Carthaginians. Hasdrubal's half-dressed, thirsty, tired and hungry troops grew hot and weary as the sun rose. Then, at noon, opening his ranks, Scipio recalled the Roman horse and skirmishers to the rear, where he kept them in reserve to support the next phase of his attack. While the Spanish mercenaries remained in the centre, Scipio and Silanus each took one wing of the army forward in two parallel columns, one of infantry, one of cavalry. As they approached Hasdrubal's line, the infantry redeployed in line to the flanks of the Roman Spanish allies, while the cavalry moved to support the flanks of the Roman infantry. The Roman formation now had its cavalry at the edges, the Spanish in the centre and the legions in between; this meant that the tough and experienced legionaries faced the edges of Hasdrubal's army, which were manned by Spanish mercenaries – his weakest troops. In the centre, Scipio ordered his own Spanish troops to hang back and take their time, dragging the Roman formation into a concave shape. As a result, Hasdrubal's best infantry in the centre were forced to wait for the Spaniards to attack even while the edges of the Roman army were striking at the Carthaginian flanks. They could not leave to help, because this would open a hole in the Carthaginian line, but nor could they go on the attack themselves, because this would expose their own flanks to assault from the Roman legionaries. Scipio had taken Hasdrubal's best troops out of the fight.

The 'Cannae in reverse' at Ilipa swallowed Hasdrubal's force in an enormous bow formation, just as the Roman army had been consumed in 216.[121] It was a tremendous testament to Scipio's achievements with his training programme. Seeing their flanks fold under the attack of Scipio's confident legionaries, and unable to attack effectively the troops in front of them, the Carthaginian veterans gave way, and when the elephants panicked, the entire Carthaginian force disintegrated. Hasdrubal managed to escape, and after a desperate running fight with Roman skirmishers and cavalry, he reached

Gades. Mago also evaded capture, but the collapse in Carthaginian fortunes was total.[122]

In just five years, Scipio had turned an imminent Roman defeat in Spain into a stunning victory. Ironically, he had achieved this largely by using the same approach with which Hannibal had persevered in Italy. By repeatedly defeating the Carthaginian armies in Spain, he had shown the leaders of the Spanish communities that they were better off with Roman friends than Carthaginian overlords. Part of the success was due to Scipio's magnanimous approach in victory. His was a diplomatic success as much as military one, but the battlefield triumphs were nonetheless essential to prove the point, and it is for his training of the army that Scipio is deservedly celebrated.

The Roman constitution normally reserved legionary command for consuls, and occasionally for their immediate subordinates, praetors. The scope of the Hannibalic War had loosened these restrictions. Successful consuls occasionally stayed in command as proconsuls past the one-year time limit of their office, and numerous other aristocrats found themselves as proconsuls or propraetors in control of the various Roman armies stationed throughout the Mediterranean. These changes created the opportunity for Roman generals to build a strong relationship with their troops and train them according to their own tactical viewpoints. Arguably, however, it was Scipio – among all of the fine generals that Rome produced during this period – who really seized this opportunity, particularly in advancing tactical thinking well beyond traditional Roman battlefield doctrine. Even if they were inspired by Cannae, the flanking and envelopment manoeuvres at Baecula and Ilipa, and the use of deception as a tool on the battlefield, were highly innovative for the Roman military. Scipio also tightly bonded his troops to his leadership, turning his army into the sort of veteran force that Hannibal had used so effectively in Italy. Another crucial improvement that Scipio made in Spain was in the effectiveness of the cavalry. In Italy, the Roman cavalry had easily been neutralised by Hannibal's Numidian horse. Indeed, many Roman troopers had actually dismounted from their horses to fight on foot, and the 'shock value' of the cavalry was minimal.[123] Yet the cavalry was valuable for flanking and envelopment, as Hannibal had shown, and if the enemy cavalry could be forced from the field, or troopers could be concealed in an opportune place, horsemen could deliver a stunning blow at the right moment. Hannibal had shown this at the Trebia and at Cannae. At Zama (202), the superiority in Roman cavalry would be an important factor in his defeat.

Greatly boosting Scipio's fortunes, adding to his cavalry strength, and further underscoring his success in Spain, was a high-profile defection in the immediate aftermath of Ilipa. Masinissa came over to Scipio, bringing with him his highly prized horsemen.[124] Scipio opened negotiations with another of Carthage's key Numidian allies, Syphax, hoping to lure him to the Roman side as well. Syphax would only meet Scipio in person, and so the Roman general, at some risk, sailed to meet him in Africa. There, he

POCKET GIANTS **HANNIBAL AND SCIPIO**

unexpectedly found Hasdrubal in harbour, but in a rather odd turn of events, Syphax imposed a truce and feasted the two generals side by side. Livy says that Hasdrubal was charmed by Scipio; so was Syphax, who turned to Rome and became Scipio's ally – for the moment.[125]

The remainder of Scipio's time in Spain was consumed with a range of small operations. Pacification proved difficult, and there was at least one brutal massacre, at Illurgia. Afterwards, a period of illness confined Scipio to his quarters. Combined with the lengthy period of campaigning in Spain, the difficulty of paying the troops and a rebellion by Mandonius and Indibilis, a mutiny broke out among some of the Roman legionaries. A weakened Scipio put down the rebellion by flogging and decapitating its ringleaders, after an impassioned speech in which he alternately shamed and praised his men.[126] It was a dirty end to a tough and relentless campaign.

5

Africa

The greatest soldiers of their time.

Livy, 30.30

Scipio defeated the rebel army of Mandonius and Indibilis in 206/5. Before returning to Rome, he founded a military colony north of Gades in which to settle some of the veterans of his campaigns. Called 'Italica', this first of Rome's overseas military colonies was the birthplace of the emperors Trajan, Hadrian and Theodosius I.

Scipio returned to Rome and met with the Senate in 205. There he reported on his successes in Spain, gave up his *imperium* and handed over the plunder from the Spanish campaign to the Roman treasury. Scipio's war record soon saw him elected consul: Livy says that in these elections the crowd was bigger than ever, and the citizens of Rome jostled with one another to catch a glimpse of the great hero.[127] As it became clear that the war was drawing to a close, some in Rome, such as Fabius Maximus and Fulvius Flaccus, pushed for the final defeat of Hannibal in Italy; others, such as Scipio, wanted to end the war with an invasion of Africa. Fabius argued that Hannibal was weak, and all of Rome's resources could be brought to bear against him. He pointed to the union of Livius and Nero against Hasdrubal (207) as a recent example of what could be accomplished. In riposte, Scipio delivered a simple argument: it was Africa's turn to be devastated. Unsettling questions, however, were being asked about

Scipio's ambition. Did he want a war in Africa for Rome – or for himself? And what about Roman strategy? Should the state remain focused on Italy, leaving Carthage more or less intact? Or should the war be taken to Africa to defeat Carthage completely, stripping it down to a mere city to secure Rome's regional interests? If Carthage was toppled, and Rome left supreme in the west, there would be little to stop Rome coming into conflict sooner or later with the major powers of the east, such as the kingdoms of Syria and Egypt.[128] The debate over how to end the war was therefore also something of a debate about the future of Rome's place in the world. While Fabius and his 'isolationist' allies in the Senate seemed content to think only in terms of Italy, Scipio's argument for an African war looked into the future, imagining Roman rule over the entire Mediterranean.[129]

Under pressure from the aristocratic faction that supported the Cornelii Scipiones, the Senate fudged all of these issues entirely by assigning one consul to Sicily, with permission to cross to Africa if it was in the 'national interest'. The other would face Hannibal in Bruttium. As the other consul, Crassus, was the chief priest (the *pontifex maximus*), who could not legally leave Italy, it was obvious who was going where, but, according to Livy, the Senate left a sting in the tail by only providing a tiny force for Sicily that was too small to invade Africa. While there are conflicting versions of this story, Livy rather credibly says that the problem was solved by Scipio's immense fame and popularity. Volunteers flocked to him, and the communities of Italy provided ships, clothing, food and all the necessary materiel for the coming conflict.[130] In the meantime, Mago, Hannibal's brother, was belatedly sent to Italy to raise rebellion in the north; he would be unsuccessful and was defeated not long afterwards in 203, dying of his wounds onboard a transport ship destined for home.

Before long the Roman vanguard, under Laelius, was in Africa, and Carthage descended into panic. Scipio had been delayed in making the crossing because of an attempt by his enemies in the Senate to have him stripped of his command. He was accused by the Fabian faction of being ultimately responsible for the depredations of a Roman officer in the city of Locri, in southern Italy, and rumours also circulated that Scipio had become 'too Greek' in Sicily, dressing in local clothes and losing his mettle for the war.[131] A senatorial commission sent to discover the truth found Scipio putting the army and navy through their paces, and, for the time being, the affair blew over. One other piece of bad news surfaced: Syphax had been lured back to the Carthaginian fold and had sealed the bargain by marrying Sophonisba, the daughter of Hasdrubal.[132] Masinissa remained in alliance with the Romans, but for the moment was locked in a bitter dynastic struggle for his throne. Eventually he prevailed, and his participation in the final offensive against his former masters was key to Scipio's victory.

The full Roman expeditionary force landed in 204 and established itself at Castra Cornelia (the 'Cornelian Camp'), close to the city of Utica. By then, Scipio's consulship was over, but his command was extended for the duration of the campaign. The Roman force was joined by a haggard Masinissa and a weary contingent of his troops. The remainder of the year passed in inconclusive skirmishing and a failed siege of Utica, which did little to improve Scipio's image among his enemies in Rome. Over the winter, Scipio tried to win Syphax back from Hasdrubal, but the Numidian refused, arguing instead, with backing from aristocrats in both Rome and Carthage, that the war should end with mutual evacuations of Africa and Italy, respectively.[133] Negotiations were failing, and Scipio needed a victory to stop his campaign from fizzling out.

The breakthrough came in 203 with a characteristically daring assault in which Scipio succeeded in driving much of the army of Hasdrubal and Syphax to flight. Spies had been secreted into the numerous delegations that had been 'discussing' peace terms with Syphax, and Scipio had learned that the housing in the Carthaginian winter camps, only about 10 miles from Castra Cornelia, was mostly built of combustible materials. Repeated meetings enabled Scipio to build up a detailed picture of his enemies, while the length of the negotiations lulled Hasdrubal and Syphax into a false sense of security. As a result, they were utterly unprepared when Scipio and Laelius, along with Masinissa, assaulted and fired the camps as their inhabitants slept. Scipio was acting more and more like Hannibal; this sort of deception, and the clever use of intelligence about the enemy, were hallmarks of Hannibal's most spectacular successes in Italy.[134]

The people of Carthage felt certain they would be assaulted next; yet surprisingly Scipio returned to his laborious siege of Utica, which allowed Hasdrubal and Syphax to raise a new army.[135] Eventually Scipio realised the danger that they posed. Leaving a force to maintain pressure on Utica, he marched rapidly to intercept Hasdrubal at a place known to history as the 'Great Plains'. In the ensuing battle, the Carthaginian force was annihilated. Two key factors in this victory were the destruction of the enemy cavalry force, and an elaborate encircling manoeuvre carried out by the rear ranks of the Roman line while the front ranks fixed the enemy in place – further practise of the tactics pioneered in the Spanish war.[136] Incredibly, Hasdrubal and Syphax escaped once again.[137]

In the aftermath of the Battle of the Great Plains, the Carthaginian Senate – seemingly galvanised to fight – ordered Hannibal to return from Italy. Not long afterwards, though, Laelius captured Syphax, and Carthaginian enthusiasm waned. An embassy was sent to Scipio to sue for peace. The delegation openly blamed Hannibal and the Barcid faction for the war, disavowing all responsibility on the part of Carthage itself. After a string of spectacular military victories, Scipio now had the chance to bolster his triumph with a harsh negotiated peace that would guarantee the primacy of the Roman state and win for himself the political glory and social renown that were the desire of all Roman aristocrats.[138] He offered terms under an armistice: Carthage would pay a heavy indemnity, would lose almost all of its remaining navy and would cede all overseas territory to Rome. The Carthaginians immediately agreed and sent an embassy to Rome to ratify the treaty. A triumphant Laelius delivered a deflated Syphax to the Senate, along with a glowing report on Scipio's success.[139] The war was over. Or was it?

It was a complex time, full of opaque political double-dealings and mixed messages. Shortly before Hannibal sailed for Carthage, the Carthaginian peace delegation arrived in Rome. It repeated its claims about Barcid responsibility for the war.[140] The sources do not agree, however, whether the peace was fully ratified. Modern historians believe this confusion to be deliberate, with later Roman writers preferring the more triumphant 'alternative ending' of the story at Zama, and wanting to make the Senate appear reluctant to end the war without a decisive African victory.[141]

While the Senate discussed terms with the Carthaginian delegation, Hasdrubal's forces in Africa captured a number of Roman resupply transports that had been blown off course and run aground. This act violated the armistice with Scipio, who now dispatched three envoys to Carthage to recover the cargoes; if everything was returned, they said, all would be forgiven. Meeting with a hostile reception, the envoys were forced to leave under the protection of a Carthaginian naval escort. But when the latter withdrew, the Roman ship carrying the envoys was attacked by Carthaginian vessels, and most of the Roman marines onboard were killed. Polybius suggests that all this was deliberate, since Hannibal's return had once again tipped the balance in favour of the hawks in the Carthaginian Senate.[142] A final showdown rapidly became inevitable.

The Battle of Zama (202) was a strange climax to an epic struggle. In the summer, with all hope of renewing the armistice lost, Scipio marched into the interior, devastating the countryside. He recalled Masinissa, who had emerged triumphant in his struggles and was busy consolidating control over his kingdom. Hannibal also moved inland from his landfall at Hadrumetum and camped at Zama, well to the south-west of Carthage. Hannibal sent out scouts to determine Scipio's location and disposition. Three were captured, and the (probably fictional) story goes that Scipio allowed them to see his camp and his preparations, and then returned them to his adversary.[143] By then Masinissa and his horsemen had arrived to reinforce Scipio's army. Hannibal, whose cavalry was neither numerous nor of high quality, would be forced to fight at a serious disadvantage. Cavalry had been decisive in his past victories over Roman forces.[144]

Both Polybius and Livy recount a meeting between Hannibal and Scipio before the battle; the story was probably invented, but made for the sort of good moralising drama essential for Livy's historical project.[145] According to their accounts, Hannibal broke the silence with an elegant request for peace. Appealing to the vicissitudes of fortune, Hannibal called on Scipio not to let his own success turn sour, as Hannibal himself had done. Scipio responded harshly by saying that the request for peace – coming as it did after the violation of the armistice – was too late, and he delivered an ultimatum:

surrender now, or fight the Roman army to the death.[146] Of course, Hannibal chose battle, and thus after sixteen years the outcome of the war hung in the balance one final time as the two giants of the conflict squared up against one another. The struggle that followed was a static, brutal affair, with little tactical sophistication. Both generals seem to have anticipated the plans of the other: Hannibal expected that Scipio would try a flanking manoeuvre of the type used at Ilipa, so he kept his third line, his veterans, well back from the front ranks. If Scipio tried to bring his troops round the edges of the Carthaginian formation, this third line would destroy them.[147] Scipio hoped to prevent his own force being enveloped by drawing Hannibal's dangerous war elephants harmlessly through his formation, and then using his superior cavalry to keep Hannibal's horses at bay. With each general divining the plans of the other, both sides were forced to opt for a bludgeoning frontal assault – an ironic outcome to a war noted for its tactical innovation and use of deception and guile on the battlefield.[148]

Scipio's confident army included the troops from the punishment brigades, the survivors of Cannae, who now redeemed themselves as they attacked and destroyed Hannibal's first two lines. The terrified survivors of the Roman assault clashed with the Carthaginian veterans in the third line as they desperately tried to escape the slaughter. The exhausted Roman troops regrouped amid piles of dead bodies, on ground slippery with blood and blocked by discarded equipment and stricken animals, and then they advanced on Hannibal's veterans. An inconclusive struggle followed, and the outcome was uncertain until Laelius and Masinissa, who commanded the Roman cavalry, drove the inexperienced Carthaginian troopers from the battlefield. With the enemy cavalry beaten, Laelius and Masinissa turned to attack Hannibal's veterans from the rear, and Carthaginian resistance collapsed.[149]

The Battle of Zama was over: Hannibal had finally been defeated.

6

Hannibal and Scipio

The Carthaginians fighting for their own safety and the dominion of Africa, and the Romans for the empire of the world.

Polybius, 15.9

Hannibal escaped the disaster at Zama. After admitting to the Carthaginian Senate that all was lost, he advised surrender. Scipio, uninterested in a costly siege of Carthage, was also willing to accept a peace deal.[150] The terms of the peace were similar to those agreed before Zama, but now included the burning of the Carthaginian navy, an act carried out by Scipio in full view of the broken and defeated population of the city. Carthage, nominally independent, was forced to acknowledge the power of Masinissa's kingdom of Numidia. In Rome, Scipio was a hero: he paid a bonus to his troops from the plunder of the war and took the name 'Africanus' in celebration of his great victories there.

Polybius claimed that the Romans fought Zama for 'world empire', and in many ways he turned out to be correct.[151] Carthage, the only state that could withstand Rome in the west, was thoroughly beaten. Macedonia's involvement meant that, by 200, Roman armies were operating in force on the Greek mainland. States fearful of Macedonia, such as the island of Rhodes and the city of Pergamum, in modern-day western Turkey, strengthened their ties with Rome, which became increasingly drawn into eastern Mediterranean affairs. In 197, a Roman army crushed the forces of Philip V at Cynoscephalae in

Thessaly, and Roman ambitions later drifted towards the Levant and Ptolemaic Egypt. The Hannibalic War set the stage for the great Roman expansion eastwards, and the ultimate creation of the Roman Empire.

Hannibal and Scipio both played roles in this crucial post-war phase. Hannibal remained in Carthage, where he stayed in command of the army for a while. Later, in 196, he was elected to the position of suffete (magistrate) in the city and undertook vital financial reforms that dramatically improved the economic health of the state.[152] His populist agenda earned him enemies among the so-called 'judges', who had replaced the Barcids as the dominant political faction, and this group now complained to Rome that he was conspiring against the Republic. Scipio came to Hannibal's defence, arguing that it was beneath Roman dignity to listen to such rumours, but he was again the target of Roman aristocratic jealousies.[153] Before long, a Roman delegation travelled to Carthage to address 'border issues'; getting wind of their real mission, Hannibal fled to the court of the Syrian monarch Antiochus III. A man of great ambition, Antiochus was increasingly embroiled in conflict with Rome over spheres of influence in the Mediterranean. Sensing the mood, Hannibal offered to serve the king against the Romans, using the tale of his long-held hatred of Rome to establish his *bona fides*.[154] Antiochus required little incentive to welcome Hannibal into his court.[155]

To this, the final part of Hannibal's life, belongs a curious anecdote about a meeting with Scipio at Ephesus, while the Roman statesman was there as a member of a

Roman delegation. According to the story, Scipio asked Hannibal who was the greatest general in history. The Carthaginian decided on Alexander, with Pyrrhus in second place. In third:

> ... myself; for when I was a young man I conquered Spain and crossed the Alps with an army, the first after Hercules. I invaded Italy and struck terror into all of you, laid waste 400 of your towns, and often put your city in extreme peril, all this time receiving neither money nor reinforcements from Carthage.[156]

His feathers ruffled, Scipio is reported to have asked Hannibal where he would rate himself if he had beaten Scipio at Zama. 'At the top', Hannibal graciously replied.[157] Was the story true? Some suggest that perhaps the conversation took place with a different Roman official, who was later replaced in the story by Scipio.[158]

Amid the political fallout from the defeat of the Macedonians in 197, Hannibal urged Antiochus to allow him to raise an army to invade Italy, and he even sent an agent to Carthage to stir up trouble there.[159] Nothing came of this, and in 190, Hannibal witnessed the defeat of the Syrian fleet by Rome's ally, Rhodes. In the same year, the Romans overwhelmed Antiochus at Magnesia in Turkey, and Hannibal's last adventure had come to an end. Short on options, he fled once again. He seems to have ended up in Armenia and Crete at different times, but nothing is sure; later, he emerged at the court of Prusias I of Bithynia, a kingdom in Turkey, where he appears to have fought on the king's side against Rome's mercurial friend Eumenes II of Pergamum.[160] During this period of his life, several ancient authors credit Hannibal with founding at least two cities, Artaxata in Armenia, and Prusa in Bithynia. From Bithynia, he warned the Rhodians in a letter against becoming too close to the Romans: prescient advice, as Rhodes would later pay terribly for being 'too helpful' in Rome's wars.[161] A manuscript purporting to be from Hannibal to the Athenians, forecasting the end of the increasingly predatory Roman presence in Greece, is also known; it is unlikely to be from Hannibal, but should perhaps be seen as an indication of the long-lived effects of Hannibal's liberation propaganda, in the context of Greek anxiety over Roman intentions towards Greece.[162] Eventually, the Romans discovered the location of their old foe, and in 183, they demanded that Prusias hand him over. The king, feeling the weight of Roman pressure, gave in. As Roman men bore down on Hannibal, the once great Carthaginian general found his escape blocked by troops, and he committed suicide.[163]

Scipio, likewise, met an end that was in jarring contrast to his illustrious military career. After Zama, he returned to a Rome that was increasingly different from the state which went confidently into the war in 218. Rome had lost much of the old aristocracy on the battlefield, and more importantly, it now found itself unchallenged in the west. As a result, Rome had a won a major stake in Mediterranean power politics, and found itself on much the same level as the great kingdoms of the east, such as Syria and Egypt.[164] The most important question facing Roman policymakers was how that stake would be managed; for the time being, the Senate looked to its victors, men like Scipio and his political allies, for guidance. After holding elaborate public games in thanksgiving for his victory, Scipio was elected to the senior position of censor in 199 and became the *princeps senatus*, the leading man of the Senate. Livy, third-hand via Tiberius Gracchus (the future son-in-law of Scipio and father of the well-known social revolutionaries, the Gracchi brothers, celebrated by a famous bronze double bust at the Musée d'Orsay in Paris), reports that the people wanted to make Scipio 'perpetual consul', but this seems to have more to do with the events of Livy's own time, which had witnessed the establishment of the imperial monarchy under Augustus.[165] Yet there were a number of serious threats to the victorious general. One man who looked on warily was Cato the Elder, who had made a political career fighting against what he saw as the deterioration of Roman customs and traditions. People such as Scipio, who had already been accused of 'going Greek' in Sicily, and Flamininus, another philhellene and the architect of Rome's victory over Philip V in 197, were his chief targets. Scipio's wife, Aemilia, had a reputation for dressing richly in contrast to an outdated wartime austerity law that Cato continued to defend. In 196, Scipio earned further scorn from senatorial hardliners for speaking out in defence of Hannibal.[166]

In 194, Scipio stood for the consulship and was elected. He had followed the rules, waiting the required ten years since his previous consular office (205). By that time it was common knowledge that Hannibal had gone over to Antiochus, and fear of the consequences probably helped Scipio at the ballot box.[167] Soon Rome was at war with Antiochus, and Scipio's brother Lucius served in Greece in 191. Several other members of Scipio's family won great renown during the campaign. The Roman expeditionary force defeated Antiochus' army at the legendary location of Thermopylae, where the 300 Spartans had died facing the Persian army nearly three centuries earlier. Confident, the Senate determined to take the war further east. Scipio Africanus could not be re-elected for a decade after 194, and so the war was entrusted to the consulship of Lucius, under his guidance. (The other consul was Laelius, Scipio's former lieutenant.) Here was an opportunity to secure the family's fame in accordance with established Roman tradition – through public service. A successful diplomatic campaign, bearing all the hallmarks of Scipio's experience, was waged in advance of the military confrontation with Antiochus. Roman agents won over Prusias and secured the marching route through the badlands that lay between Macedonia and Turkey. The Romans crossed the Hellespont – the first Roman army to do so – but Scipio became ill and was absent from the final battle at Magnesia, leaving his brother and his experienced generals to beat Antiochus.[168]

In the aftermath of the Roman victory, opposition to the Scipios, led by Cato, gradually solidified around jealousy of their success and resentment at their apparent love of Greek culture, which greatly offended the traditionalists. A speech made by Lucius in the Senate about his victory was met from some quarters with disparaging comments that Thermopylae, where Cato had fought, had been more important than Magnesia.[169] Much, though, is unclear; Livy himself said that none of his sources for this senatorial intrigue perfectly aligned with each other.[170] Whatever the precise sequence of events, Scipio and his allies were slowly squeezed out, and attacks on them mounted. At some point around 188 or 187, Lucius was accused of embezzlement on the campaign against Antiochus; 'abuse of public funds' was a well-worn tactic in Greek and Roman politics. In front of the Senate, Scipio ripped up the accounts, telling the prosecutor to search among the tiny pieces of paper if he wanted to know more. Lucius was eventually saved from prison by Tiberius Gracchus, although a hefty fine was imposed.[171]

Political attacks continued, however, culminating in the inconclusive prosecution of Scipio on trumped-up charges of accepting bribes during campaign against Antiochus. The prosecution even wheeled out the old accusations laid against him while he was in Syracuse, preparing for the war in Africa. Faced again by the faction of Cato, Scipio, accompanied by a sympathetic crowd, avoiding talking about the charges and instead invoked his war record and the reputation of his family. Such a tactic did not inspire complete confidence in Scipio's innocence, but some, Livy says, thought the whole affair to be thoroughly shameful – how could Rome cast out Scipio, the man who had saved it from destruction? Scipio tried to rescue the situation with an ostentatious public sacrifice at the Temple of Jupiter, his old benefactor, but his aura was fading. Old and ill, he retired to an austere villa at Liternum in Campania.[172] Livy says that success had gone to his head, and he was unable to see why he might need to plead his case. During the final round of legal proceedings, he claimed ill health and did not appear in court. Another view is expressed by Tiberius Gracchus, who asserted that Scipio's service to the state deserved better treatment.[173] Yet before long Scipio died, effectively an exile, discarded by a feckless and factional society, and Scipio's enemies in the Senate continued to attack his reputation even after he had been buried.[174]

7

Legacy

We cannot but justly admire Hannibal.

Scipio, as I have said, was exceptionally painstaking and at the same time very sagacious and practical.

Polybius, 11.19 and 11.24

Polybius praised Hannibal for holding together a multi-ethnic force which brought one of the most formidable military powers of antiquity to the edge of extinction.[175] Writing in the first century BC, Diodorus Siculus, drawing on Polybius' assessment, concluded his appreciation of Hannibal's exploits with a flattering verdict on his leadership: 'all may read the lesson that the commander is to an army what the mind is to the body, and is responsible for its success.'[176] Diodorus also admired Scipio, noting that through 'artful planning, without battle or risk', he compelled Hannibal to abandon Italy, and then, at Zama, became the first to defeat him comprehensively in battle.[177]

The achievements of Hannibal and Scipio resonated well beyond the writers of antiquity. Sir Basil Liddell-Hart rated Scipio as a greater general than Napoleon, while the great French leader was himself inspired by Hannibal's stunning successes. The tactics used at Cannae also won the praise of Montgomery of Alamein and influenced Wellington, the Schlieffen Plan, Rommel's war in Africa and the invasion of Iraq in 1991.[178] Hannibal and Scipio have also made their mark on popular culture, with the former used to market Pimm's (!), and the story of both framing the plot of several films from the twentieth century.[179] Artists from the medieval period onwards have used stories from the Hannibalic War to inspire their work, and Scipio and Hannibal naturally made their mark on the literary scene. In antiquity the poets Ennius and Silius Italicus put Scipio's success into verse, and Scipio would later inspire both Dante and Petrarch. In the seventeenth century, Thomas Nabbes penned a tragic drama, *Hannibal and Scipio*, which took a Livian approach to the rivalry between the two men. The literary legacy of Hannibal appears most famously, perhaps, in the *Aeneid*, the great Roman 'national' epic. In Book 4, Dido, Queen of Carthage, foretells Carthage's future vengeance, anticipating the birth of Hannibal and his invasion of Italy. It is one of history's marvellous ironies that Carthage would in fact gain a second vengeance, when Gaiseric, King of the Vandals, who had captured most of Roman North Africa in the early fifth century AD, sailed from Carthage to Rome in AD 455 and thoroughly sacked the city.

One of the advantages of placing Hannibal and Scipio side by side is to note how each affected the other; the two men are, in fact, remarkably similar. Perhaps the most intriguing 'cross-pollination' between the two is found in the way that Hannibal seems to have stimulated the 'rise of the individual' in the rather corporate world of Roman politics. Hannibal was a visionary and talented individual who collided with a state whose strength was traditionally vested in its institutions. Even with the sterling contributions of the *Senatus Populusque Romanus* – the Senate and the Roman people – the Republic only *really* prevailed when it offered up, in return, an individual of similar imagination and greatness. Stories of Scipio's links to the divine mirror those of Hannibal; his leadership skills and qualities, and his ability to inspire men, were similar to Hannibal's; his tactical insights and capacity to improvise and use deception on the battlefield were comparable to those of Hannibal; and Scipio's determination to detach allies from Carthage during the Spanish campaign reflected Hannibal's own efforts in Italy.

In the world of Roman politics, though, Scipio's tendency towards individualism was not welcome. Diodorus observed that 'because of his great achievements Scipio wielded more influence than seemed compatible with the dignity of the state'.[180] Prior to the Hannibalic War, the Roman constitution had managed to channel aristocratic ambition into state service. Traditionalists could point to the great consuls and dictators of the past such as Cincinnatus, who performed their duty and laid down their office when their time was up. Certainly, Scipio, who had broken constitutional rules repeatedly during the war, was careful not to do so afterwards. Personal ambitions could still be restrained by the post-war Senate and its defenders, who remained strong for many decades to come. Yet the conflict that proved the resilience of the Senate simultaneously created a great general who cultivated a close personal link to his soldiers, who was immensely popular with the voters, who allowed rumours of divine support to flourish, and who personally paid his troops bonuses from plunder seized in innumerable victories. Without the oversight of a powerful Senate, this type of man might have become a warlord – indeed, later, and unfettered by the inconvenience of well-defended constitutional rules, such men *did* become warlords: Marius, Sulla, Julius Caesar, Pompey, Antony and Octavian (Augustus). Scipio achieved much that was against the *mos maiorum*, the customs of the state and its elders, by recourse to popular support.[181] While nearly two centuries separate the Hannibalic War from the victory of Augustus, it was clear even in antiquity that the confrontation between Hannibal and Scipio created dangerous uncertainties in Roman politics. It was equally clear to people like Polybius that the war had also opened up the Mediterranean to unrestrained Roman ambition. The rivalry between Hannibal and Scipio laid the foundation for the spread of Roman power from northern England to the Middle East, profoundly affecting almost every aspect of our civilisation. It is a legacy that still resonates today.

Notes

1   Polybius, 2.20.

2   Fronda, M., 'Hannibal: Tactics, Strategy, and Geostrategy', in D. Hoyos (ed.), *A Companion to the Punic Wars* (Wiley-Blackwell, 2011), pp. 242–59, at p. 257.

3   Cf. Fronda, 'Hannibal', p. 258.

4   Livy, 38.50.

5   Miles, R., 'Hannibal and Propaganda' in Hoyos, *Companion*, pp. 260–79, at p. 261.

6   See Mineo, B., 'Principal Literary Sources for the Punic Wars (Apart from Polybius)', in Hoyos, *Companion*, pp. 111–28.

7   Champion, C., 'Polybius and the Punic Wars', in Hoyos, *Companion*, pp. 95–110.

8   Mineo, 'Principal Literary Sources'; Garland, R., *Hannibal* (Bristol Classical Press, 2010), 30–7; D. Hoyos, *Hannibal: Rome's Greatest Enemy* (Liverpool University Press, 2008), pp. 3–8.

9   Polybius, 3.20.

10   Ibid., 3.11–12; Nepos, *Hannibal*, 2.

11   Polybius, 3.8, citing Fabius Pictor.

12   Beck, H., 'The Reasons for the War', in Hoyos, *Companion*, pp. 225–41, at 234.

13   Barceló, P., 'Punic Politics, Economy, and Alliances, 218–201', in Hoyos, *Companion*, pp. 357–75, at p. 361.

14   Polybius, 3.30.

15   Ibid., 2.13. See also Beck, 'The Reasons', pp. 237–40.

16   Zimmerman, K., 'Roman Strategy and aims in the Second

Punic War', in Hoyos, *Companion*, 280–98, at p. 283.

17 Polybius, 2.36.

18 Beck, 'The Reasons', p. 230.

19 Ibid., pp. 230–1; Zimmerman, 'Roman Strategy', pp. 281–2.

20 Livy, 21.14.

21 Polybius, 9.22.

22 Nepos, *Hannibal*, 13.

23 Dio, 13.54.

24 Livy, 21.4.

25 Polybius, 3.14.

26 Ibid., 3.48.

27 Ibid., 3.54–5; Nepos, *Hannibal*, 1, 4–5.

28 Livy, 21.4; Silius Italicus, Punica, 1.56–60.

29 Polybius, 3.15.

30 Ibid., 9.25.

31 Ibid., 2.24.

32 Rosenstein, N., *Rome and the Mediterranean, 290 to 146 BC: The Imperial Republic* (Edinburgh University Press, 2012), p. 73, following P.A. Brunt.

33 Polybius 3.56.

34 Plutarch, Pyrrhus, 25.5.

35 Fronda, 'Hannibal', p. 250.

36 Ibid., p. 256.

37 Miles, 'Hannibal and Propaganda', pp. 265–79.

38 Polybius, 3.48.

39 Ibid.; see Proctor, D., Hannibal's March in History (Oxford University Press, 1971).

40 Livy, 21.29.

41 Ibid., 21.33.

42 Ibid., 21.28.

43 Ibid., 21.37; Nepos, *Hannibal*, 3.

44 Polybius 3.62; Rawlings, L., 'The War in Italy, 218–203'; in Hoyos, *Companion*, pp. 299–319, at p. 305.

45 Livy, 21.42–3.

46 Ibid., 21.46.

47 Fronda, 'Hannibal', p. 245.

48 Livy, 21.54.

49 Appian, *Hannibalic War*, 7.

50 Livy, 21.63.

51 Gabriel, R., *Scipio Africanus: Rome's Greatest General* (Potomac Books Inc., 2008), p. 39.

52 Livy, 22.2.

53 Ibid., 22.4–8.

54 Polybius, 3.93–4; Fronda, 'Hannibal', 245.

55 Appian, *Hannibalic War*, 16.

56 Ammianus, 31.13.

57 Appian, *Hannibalic War*, 18–26.

58 Ibid., 23.

59 Livy, 22.61.

60 Ibid., 22.49.

61 Ibid., 22.53.

62 Ibid., 22.51.

63 Ibid.; Hoyos, *Hannibal*, 60.

64 Livy, 30.20.

65 Garland, *Hannibal*, p. 93.

66 Hoyos, *Hannibal*, pp. 60–1.

67 Fronda, 'Hannibal', p. 249.

68 Livy, 22.58; Fronda, M., *Between Rome and Carthage: Southern Italy During the Second Punic War* (Cambridge University Press, 2010), pp. 34–5.

69 Beck, 'The Reasons', p. 228; Fronda, *Between Rome and Carthage*, p. 35.

70   Fronda, 'Hannibal', p. 252.

71   Ibid., p. 253; Plutarch, *Pyrrhus*, 18.

72   Livy, 22.58.

73   Ibid., 22.61.

74   Polybius, 2.24.

75   Ibid., 9.26; Fronda, *Between Rome and Carthage*; Rawlings, 'The War in Italy', p. 312.

76   Plutarch, *Pyrrhus*, 21.10.

77   Zimmerman, 'Roman Strategy', p. 286–7.

78   Livy, 23.12.

79   Ibid., 23.12–13.

80   Ibid., 23.15; Fronda, 'Hannibal', p. 247.

81   Polybius, 3.91.

82   Livy, 23.7.

83   Ibid., 23.10.

84   Ibid., 23.19–20.

85   Ibid., 23.18; Appian, *Hannibalic War*, 43.

86   Livy, 23.44.

87   Polybius, 7.9; Fronda, 'Hannibal', p. 250.

88   Edwell, P., 'War Abroad: Spain, Sicily, Macedon, Africa', in Hoyos, *Companion*, pp. 320–38, at p. 325.

89   Livy, 26.11.

90   Plutarch, Fabius, 23.1.

91   Plutarch, Marcellus, 9.4; cf. Plutarch, *Fabius*, 19.3.

92   Livy, 27.28.

93   Ibid., 27.39.

94   Appian, *Hannibalic War*, 53; cf. Polybius, 11.1–2.

95   Livy, 27.49–51.

96   Lazenby, J., *Hannibal's War* (Aris & Phillips, 1978).

97   Polybius, 10.3.

98   Livy, 25.2.

99   Ibid., 26.18.

100 Ibid.

101 Ibid., 22.26.

102 Ibid., 26.19; Plutarch, *Alexander*, 2.6.

103 Polybius, 10.2.

104 Ibid., 10.5.

105 Livy, 26.37.

106 Appian, *Spanish War*, 19.

107 Livy, 26.41.

108 Polybius, 10.7.

109 Livy, 26.45; Polybius 10.11.

110 Livy, 26.47.

111 Ibid., 26.51.

112 Ibid., 27.17.

113 Gabriel, *Scipio*, pp. 103–4.

114 Livy, 27.18.

115 Gabriel, *Scipio*, p. 114; Scullard, H.H., *Scipio Africanus: Soldier and Politician* (Thames & Hudson Ltd, 1970), p. 73.

116 Livy, 27.19.

117 Ibid., 27.20.

118 Scullard, *Scipio*, pp. 80–1.

119 Livy, 28.3.

120 Ibid., 28.13–14; Polybius 11.22.

121 Polybius. 11.24; Gabriel, *Scipio*, p. 121.

122 Livy, 28.16.

123 Gabriel, *Scipio*, p. 118.

124 Livy, 28.17.

125 Ibid., 28.18.

126 Ibid., 28.19–21, 27–9; Polybius 11.25–30.

127 Livy, 28.38.

128 Gabriel, *Scipio*, pp. 139–40.

129 Ibid., p. 125; Scullard, *Scipio*, p. 110.

130 Livy, 28.45.

131 Ibid., 29.16–22.

132 Ibid., 29.23.

133 Gabriel, *Scipio*, p. 163.

134 Livy, 30.3–6.

135 Gabriel, *Scipio*, p. 166.

136 Ibid., p. 169.

137 Ibid., pp. 172–3; Edwell, 'War Abroad', p. 334.

138 Gabriel, *Scipio*, p. 174; Zimmerman, 'Roman Strategy', p. 294.

139 Livy, 30.17–18, 21.

140 Ibid., 30.22; Nepos, *Hannibal*, 1.

141 Edwell, 'War Abroad', p. 335; Zimmerman, 'Roman Strategy', p. 294; Hoyos, *Hannibal*, pp. 101–2; Scullard, *Scipio*, p. 136.

142 Polybius, 15.1–2.

143 Livy, 30.29; Gabriel, *Scipio*, p. 182.

144 Polybius, 15.3; Gabriel, *Scipio*, p. 183.

145 Polybius, 15.7–8; Livy, 30.30.

146 Polybius, 15.8; Livy, 30.30–3.

147 Gabriel, *Scipio*, p. 187; Scullard, *Scipio*, p. 151.

148 Gabriel, *Scipio*, p. 191; Scullard, *Scipio*, pp. 149–54.

149 Polybius, 15.14.

150 Scullard, *Scipio*, pp. 155–6.

151 Polybius, 15.9.

152 Nepos, *Hannibal*, 7.

153 Livy, 33.47.

154 Nepos, *Hannibal*, 1.

155 Appian, *Syrian Wars*, 4.

156 Ibid., 10; cf. Livy, 35.14.

157 Livy, 35.14; Appian, *Syrian Wars*, 10.

158 Hoyos, *Hannibal*, p. 133.

159 Appian, *Syrian Wars*, 7–8.

160 Nepos, *Hannibal*, 10.4–11.

161 Ibid., 10.1.

162 Garland, *Hannibal*, pp. 126–7.

163 Nepos, *Hannibal*, 13.

164 Scullard, *Scipio*, p. 173.

165 Livy, 38.56.

166 Scullard, *Scipio*, p. 188.

167 Ibid., p. 192.

168 Ibid., p. 205.

169 Livy, 37.58.

170 Ibid., 38.56.

171 Ibid., 38.55, 59.

172 Ibid., 38.50–1; Appian, *Syrian Wars*, 40.

173 Livy, 38.52–3.

174 Scullard, *Scipio*, p. 224.

175 Polybius, 11.19; cf. Livy, 28.12.

176 Diodorus, 29.19.

177 Ibid., 29.20.

178 Garland, *Hannibal*, pp. 144–5, 54; Fields, N., *Hannibal* (Osprey Publishing, 2010), p. 60.

179 Garland, *Hannibal*, pp. 145–52.

180 Diodorus, 29.21.

181 Scullard, *Scipio*, p. 239; Toynbee, A., *Hannibal's Legacy: The Hannibalic War's Effects on Roman Life* (Oxford University Press, 1965).

Timeline

All dates BC

275	Pyrrhus defeated
264	First Punic War begins
247/6	Hannibal born
241	First Punic War ends
c. 236	Scipio born
?220s	Roman agreement with Saguntum
226	'Ebro' treaty agreed
219	Hannibal's attack on Saguntum
218	Hannibalic War begins: Romans defeated at Ticinus and Trebia rivers
217	Roman defeat at Lake Trasimene
216	Roman defeat at Cannae
212	Scipio elected curule aedile
211	Elder Scipio brothers killed in Spain; Hannibal's march on Rome
210	Younger Scipio arrives in Spain; final Roman victory in Sicily
209	New Carthage captured by Scipio
208	Hasdrubal beaten at Baecula by Scipio
207	Hasdrubal killed in northern Italy
206	Hasdrubal (son of Gisgo) and Mago beaten at Ilipa by Scipio
205	Scipio elected consul

203	Battle of the Great Plains; Hannibal recalled to Africa
202	Hannibal defeated by Scipio at Zama
201	Peace between Carthage and Rome; Scipio takes title 'Africanus'
199	Scipio elected as censor and appointed *princeps senatus*
196	Hannibal elected as suffete in Carthage
195	Hannibal flees to Antiochus III
194	Scipio elected consul
187–5	Prosecution of the Scipios
c. **183**	Hannibal commits suicide; Scipio dies at Liternum (date uncertain)

Further Reading

Ancient Sources

Appian, *Roman History*, trans. H. White, 4 vols
(Cambridge, MA, 1912–13)

Cassius Dio, *Roman History*, trans. E. Cary, 9 vols
(Cambridge, MA, 1914–27)

Diodorus Siculus, *Library of History*, trans. R.M. Geer,
C.H. Oldfather, C.L. Sherman, F.R. Walton and
C.B. Welles, 12 vols (Cambridge, MA, 1933–67)

Livy, *The War with Hannibal: Books XXI–XXX of The
History of Rome from its Foundation*, trans. A. de
Sélincourt (London, 1965)

Nepos, *On Great Generals. On Historians*, trans. J.C. Rolfe
(Cambridge, MA, 1929)

Plutarch, *Lives*, trans. B. Perrin, 11 vols (Cambridge, MA,
1914–26)

Polybius, *The Histories, Books 9–15*, trans. W.R. Paton
(Cambridge, MA, 2011)

Polybius, *The Histories*, trans. R. Waterfield (Oxford,
2010)

Silius Italicus, *Punica*, trans. J. Duff, 2 vols (Cambridge,
MA, 1934)

Select Secondary Works

Bagnall, N., *The Punic Wars: Rome, Carthage, and the Struggle for the Mediterranean* (Pimlico, 1999)

Cottrell, L., *Hannibal: Enemy of Rome* (Da Capo Press, 1960)

Fields, N., *Hannibal* (Osprey Publishing, 2010)

Fronda, M., *Between Rome and Carthage: Southern Italy During the Second Punic War* (Cambridge University Press, 2010)

Goldsworthy, A.K., *The Punic Wars* (Cassell, 2000)

Gabriel, R., *Scipio Africanus: Rome's Greatest General* (Potomac Books Inc., 2008)

Gabriel, R., *Hannibal: The Military Biography of Rome's Greatest Enemy* (University of Nebraska Press, 2011)

Garland, R., *Hannibal* (Bristol Classical Press, 2010)

Hoyos, D., *Hannibal's Dynasty. Power and Politics in the Western Mediterranean, 247–138 BC* (Routledge, 2005)

Hoyos, D., *Hannibal: Rome's Greatest Enemy* (Liverpool University Press, 2008)

Hoyos, D. (ed.), *A Companion to the Punic Wars* (Wiley-Blackwell, 2011)

Lancel, S., *Hannibal* (Fayard, 1995)

Lazenby, J., *Hannibal's War* (Aris & Phillips, 1978)

Liddell Hart, Sir B.H., *Scipio Africanus: Greater than Napoleon* (Da Capo Press, 1926)

Macdonald, E., *Hannibal: A Hellenistic Life* (Yale University Press, 2015)

Peddie, J., *Hannibal's War* (Sutton Publishing Ltd, 1997)

Proctor, D., *Hannibal's March in History* (Oxford University Press, 1971)

Rosenstein, N., *Rome and the Mediterranean, 290 to 146 BC: The Imperial Republic* (Edinburgh University Press, 2012)

Scullard, H.H., *Scipio Africanus: Soldier and Politician* (Thames & Hudson Ltd, 1970)

Toynbee, A., *Hannibal's Legacy: The Hannibalic War's Effects on Roman Life* (Oxford University Press, 1965)

Web Links

www.livius.org/articles/concept/consul – For Roman consuls and their role

www.livius.org/articles/person/polybius – A biography of Polybius

www.vroma.org/~bmcmanus/romanarmy.html – The organisation of the Roman army in the late Republic and early Empire

whc.unesco.org/en/list/37– UNESCO listing for Carthage, World Heritage Site

Acknowledgements

Thanks are due to Tony Morris for the inspiration to return to my Roman Republican roots, and to Rob Boddice, Michael Fronda, Marianne Goodfellow and Stephanie Olsen for reading drafts and offering their advice and corrections.

Copyright notices
Thank you to the following for their excerpts used in this text:
Polybius, Books 1–8: reprinted by permission of OUP from Polybius, *Histories*, trans. Robin Waterfield with introduction and notes by Brian McGing (Oxford, 2010).
Polybius, Books 9–15: Polybius, *The Histories*, vol. 4, Loeb Classical Library 159, trans. W.R. Paton, rev. F.W. Walbank (Cambridge, MA, Harvard University Press © 2011).
Appian, Book 10: Appian, *Roman History*, vol. 2, Loeb Classical Library 3, trans. H. White (Cambridge, MA, Harvard University Press © 1912).
Diodorus, Book 29: Diodorus Siculus, *Library of History*, vol. XI, Loeb Classical Library 409, trans. F.R. Walton (Cambridge, MA: Harvard University Press © 1957).
Plutarch, *Life of Pyrrhus*: Plutarch, *Lives*, vol. 9, Loeb Classical Library 101, trans. B. Perrin (Cambridge, MA: Harvard University Press © 1920).

ACKNOWLEDGEMENTS

Loeb Classical Library ® is a registered trademark of the President and Fellows of Harvard College.

All other translations are by the author.

Giuseppe Verdi Henry V **Brunel** Pope John Paul II **Jane Austen** Sigmund Freud **Abraham Lincoln** Robert the Bruce **Charles Darwin** Buddha **Elizabeth I** Horatio Nelson **Wellington** Hannibal & Scipio **Jesus** Joan of Arc **Anne Frank** Alfred the Great **King Arthur** Henry Ford **Nelson Mandela** Edward Jenner **Napoleon Bonaparte** Isaac Newton **Albert Einstein** John Lennon **Elizabeth II**